"A great and wonderful book.
– Dr R T

"If you care about your children's
is essential reading. Buy one for y ..... one for the youth
worker!"
– Krish Kandiah, Executive Director: Churches in Mission,
Evangelical Alliance

"This book caused me to laugh and cry, worship and pray, and
to be both thankful and penitent. This is vintage Rob Parsons –
biblically wise, wonderfully witty, totally engaging, and full of the
warm-hearted grace of God. I loved this book and its vital message.
You will too!"
– Dr Steve Brady, Principal, Moorlands College

"I can say from hard-won experience that this book hits the spot.
Rob Parsons touches the real issues we need to face in showing our
children what God's love looks like. He gets to the heart of how
to live authentically in front of our children; he shows us how to
avoid the trap of trying to look 'respectable' while missing reality
in our relationships; and he offers practical ways to prepare our
children for life in the real world."
– Revd Ian Coffey, Speaker, author, husband,
father and grandfather

"Rob Parsons' honest, wise and practical insights will help parents
guide their children through the bumpy waters of growing up in
their local church."
– Nola Leach, General Director, CARE

Getting
Your Kids
through Church
without them
Ending up
Hating God

ROB PARSONS

MONARCH
BOOKS

Oxford, UK & Grand Rapids, Michigan, USA

First published in the UK in 2011 by Monarch Books
(a publishing imprint of Lion Hudson plc)
Wilkinson House, Jordan Hill Road, Oxford OX2 8DR, England
Tel: +44 (0)1865 302750 Fax: +44 (0)1865 302757
Email: monarch@lionhudson.com
www.lionhudson.com

ISBN 978 0 85721 053 1 (print)
ISBN 978 0 85721 115 6 (ePub)
ISBN 978 0 85721 114 9 (Kindle)
ISBN 978 0 85721 116 3 (PDF)

Published jointly with Care for the Family, Garth House,
Leon Avenue, Cardiff CF15 7RG;
www.careforthefamily.org.uk.

Distributed by:
UK: Marston Book Services, PO Box 269, Abingdon, Oxon, OX14 4YN

Unless otherwise stated, Scripture quotations taken from the Holy Bible, New International Version, copyright © 1973, 1978, 1984 by the International Bible Society. Used by permission of Zondervan and Hodder & Stoughton Limited. All rights reserved. The 'NIV' and 'New International Version' trademarks are registered in the United States Patent and Trademark Office by International Bible Society. Use of either trademark requires the permission of International Bible Society. UK trademark number 1448790. Quotatiom marked NLT taken from taken from the Holy Bible, New Living Translation, copyright © 1996, 2004, 2007 by Tyndale House Foundation. Used by permission of Tyndale House Publishers, Inc., Carol Stream, Illinois 60188. All rights reserved.

The text paper used in this book has been made from wood independently certified as having come from sustainable forests.

British Library Cataloguing Data
A catalogue record for this book is available from the British Library.

Printed and bound in Great Britain by Clays Ltd, St Ives plc.

Contents

Acknowledgments

A big thank you goes to everyone who worked on the book with me, especially Jon Matthias, who worked on it from the beginning. Thanks also to Mark Molden, June Way, Steve Williams and all the team at CFF, and to Michael Bates, Lyndon Bowring, Paul Francis, Kate Hancock, Jon Mason and Owain Williams.

My agent Eddie Bell of the Bell Lomax Agency did his usual brilliant job together with his colleagues Pat, Paul, June and Jo. Many thanks also to Tony Collins and the team at Monarch.

Special thanks to my wife, Dianne, who gave me her usual wisdom, insights and patience while I was writing.

As ever, the book wouldn't have seen the light of day without the work Sheron Rice did – once again, much appreciation to her.

Some names in the text have been changed to protect confidentiality.

❋ ❋ ❋

This book is dedicated to Mark Molden and the team he leads at Care for the Family, and to Paul and Jane Francis – thank you.

"I don't want my kids hating God because of me."

Some years ago Wayne Cordeiro, the pastor and author of the brilliant book *Leading on Empty*[1], was asked to meet with a group of American church leaders. Most were around forty years old and all had churches with over 3,000 members. On the second day of the conference the organizers asked these leaders a question that caught many of them off guard: "What do you fear the most?" Cordeiro says that as each took a turn at answering, tears began to flow and several couldn't even finish what they'd started to say. One admitted that he didn't know how much longer his marriage could sustain the pressure of his job. But it was another leader's answer that got Wayne Cordeiro's attention. His greatest fear?

"I just don't want my kids growing up hating God because of me."

I've thought so much about that church leader and what he said. I care about the local church. My wife,

Dianne, and I have only ever attended two churches in our whole lives and one of those is a plant from the other. We are in that church almost every Sunday. I used to be involved in the leadership there, but I left that role to concentrate on my work with the charity Care for the Family. When I resigned I said to the congregation, "I'm sure you'll do better without me than with me." They did. I love that place.

And I care about church leaders. During the First World War some soldiers who were sent home from the front were given the title "honourably wounded". Many of the church leaders I meet are "honourably wounded". The pressure – physical, emotional and spiritual – combined with the constant energy-sapping criticism has taken its toll. I know that church leaders aren't perfect, but we dare not take them for granted. One of the greatest privileges of my life has been the opportunity to speak with thousands of leaders across the world and try to encourage them.

But as I reflected on this man's words my heart went out to him not just as a church leader, but even more as a *parent*. I hope that this book will be of help to church leaders; however, I have written it for all kinds of mothers and fathers.

When asked about his greatest fear, the church

leader at the conference could have mentioned any one of a hundred fears to do with his job: that his church wouldn't prosper, that the funds wouldn't come in for the building programme, perhaps that one of his deacons would change his mind about retiring! But no: his first thoughts were for his children.

Why the fear that they might hate God because of him? Was he a monster at home? I'm sure he wasn't. Did he not provide for his family? I have no doubt that he did. Did he not love his children? I am sure he would have given his life for them.

I think I understand the reason why many parents have felt that fear, because the spectre of it has terrorized my own heart. It is that the experience of being brought up in a Christian home and being intimately involved in the life of a local church, with all the pressures that can bring, could damage the seeds of faith in our children's hearts. Our fear is that the exposure they have to Christianity will cause them to have little love for God or his people.

"There is no pain like parental pain."[2] So wrote psychologist John White. If he is right then it is because there is no love like parental love. We can treat our husband, wife, friends or colleagues so badly that it is possible they will stop loving us. But most parents find it

9

hard to imagine anything their child could do that would cause them to say, "I just don't love her any more."

C. S. Lewis wrote, "Love anything and your heart will be wrung and possibly broken. If you want to make sure of keeping it intact you must give it to no one, not even an animal."[3] All over the world I meet parents who are in pain for their children. On the surface it can be hard to understand why. These young people (and sometimes much older ones) may have excellent jobs and a good set of friends, and perhaps be happily married with children of their own. More than that, they are loving sons and daughters. So why then are their parents grieving? It's because, although their children were brought up in a Christian home, and although they attended church for most of their young lives, they seem to have hard hearts that are closed to faith. It's almost as if they have been inoculated against Christianity and now react negatively whenever they come into contact with it.

Who would want to be part of a faith like that?

Megan was twenty-five years old. Until the age of sixteen, every Sunday she had attended the church that her mother carried her into when she was a baby. I asked her if she went to church now and she shook her head. Her jaw tightened. "No. I don't believe any of that God stuff now." I bought her a coffee and asked her to tell me why she felt that way...

An hour later we said goodbye, and as she left I gazed after her. I knew that she felt her story was unique, and of course in some ways it was, but as I listened it seemed as if I had heard it a thousand times. It was not a story of intellectual doubt robbing her soul of faith, or of crushing persecution terrifying her heart into denial of God. It was not even a story of out-and-out rebellion – of her shaking a fist at heaven and partying to forget she had done it. No. She sighed more than ranted and quietly told me of the people, events, attitudes, and disappointments – some of them with herself – that had eventually snuffed out the flame of faith in her heart.

In the following days I found it hard to get Megan out of my mind, and I knew why. It was because of her very last comment to me. It would have been easier to take if it had been said with bitterness, but it wasn't. She said it with sad resignation. "Rob, why would anybody want to be part of a faith like that?"

Almost every parent realizes that they have made mistakes, and yet the truth is that most of us have given the task of raising our children our very best shot. We know there are a hundred things we would do differently if we could have another go – though we have a sneaking suspicion that, even then, we'd just make different mistakes.

Most of us don't need any more guilt. An old man looking back at almost three-quarters of a century of fatherhood said, "Parenting is fifty per cent fear and fifty per cent guilt." I agree – except I think he's probably a little light on the guilt side. So many parents live with guilt. At times it suffocates us, enslaves us, and finally it consumes us. We feel totally responsible for the actions and attitudes of our children.

Logic doesn't help. The fact that our son is now a thirty-seven-year-old lumberjack with four kids of his own doesn't stop us wondering whether, if we'd pushed him a bit harder with his homework when he was thirteen, he would now be a brain surgeon. One woman wrote to me and said, "Guilt comes attached to the placenta." But guilt like that rarely helps us, and sometimes we have to remember that even God has trouble with his children.

My own children are now grown and married and I thank God for what he's done in their lives. But there have been many tears along the way, some "if onlys", and while perhaps no "haunting regrets", nevertheless a wish that when Dianne and I first became parents somebody had at least warned us about some of the issues that we'll consider together in this book. It matters.

When you pray for your children, ask God to protect them from the dozens of pitfalls that await them in life: greed, easy sex, illicit drugs, alcohol abuse, and a hundred other traps. Ask him to help them as they face those who would ridicule their faith and trash it before their eyes. If persecution comes to them, pray that they will have the courage to face it. But, when you have done all that, pray about another danger – the thing that destroys the seed of faith in millions of young people: ask that your children may come through their early experience of Christianity without them ending up hating God.

I realize that this may not seem a very ambitious prayer. I understand that your heartfelt prayer is that they will end up *loving* God – of course. Nevertheless, there are millions of parents who would settle for an adult child who at least had a heart that was still open to God.

But, before we start, let me say this. If our children are grown, it may be hard to read a book like this because we feel that perhaps for us it's too late. If this is your situation, let me remind you of that wonderful verse from the book of Joel: "I will give you back the years the

13

locusts have eaten."[4] It is never too late to reach out to an adult child; never too late to say sorry; never too late to pray.

Over the past ten years I have spoken to tens of thousands of people across the world at "Bringing Home the Prodigals" events. And I have discovered that many "prodigals" never did turn their back on God – they rejected something else. This book is an exploration of what that *something* may be. And if we can discover that "something", then perhaps we can prevent many children from going down the same route. And perhaps we can even realize that many of our so-called "prodigals" are not as far from God as we thought.

Chapter 1

God has No Grandchildren

As I write, it is mid-December and if all goes to plan I am just a few weeks away from being a grandfather – a little one is due to join our family sometime over Christmas. This will be a new experience for me, and actually rather interesting, because it's where I get the chance even to steal a march on God.

We all know that time and time again when the New Testament writers searched their minds for a word to describe God's relationship to us, it is the word "Father" that they chose. In fact that is often the word that Jesus himself used of God. But God will never be a grandfather – simply because he has no grandchildren. Everyone who enters a relationship with him does so directly as a son or daughter. Parents may have a strong faith and may do their best to pass it on to their children by teaching and example, but they can only go so far in that. If their children are to have a real faith, they must grasp, receive and experience it *for themselves*.

A friend of mine was once asked to give a talk entitled "How to Bring up Godly Children". Only somebody who has no children, whose kids are under seven years old, or who has four offspring who think church is more fun than *The Simpsons* could dream up such a title. The truth is that there is no "How to..." manual that can guarantee we will bring up godly children. The best we can do is to try to influence them by living a godly life. But even there we will fail – and for that very reason generations of parents have fallen to their knees before God for their children.

We can – and must – do things, pass on values, and demonstrate attitudes that will make it easier for our children to develop a relationship with God. But what you and I cannot do is bear *total responsibility* for their spiritual journey.

I know there is that lovely verse from the book of Proverbs: "Train a child in the way he should go, and when he is old he will not turn from it,"[1] but this is a principle, not a guarantee. As parents we can influence, advise, mentor, pray, and sometimes drag kids to church when they don't want to go. But what we cannot do is bear the responsibility of bringing up godly children.

Now if you have three children who are all "godly", I don't blame you for thinking it's due to the way you brought them up. But the truth is that, although your wonderful parenting helped, there are thousands of parents who did just as good a job as you, but whose kids have gone right off the rails. And, as I have mentioned before, even God – the perfect father – has trouble with his children.

But trying to bring up godly children is what so many of us do. And, actually, what we so often achieve is a *semblance* of godliness that lasts for a while, but is only skin deep. It's as if we are trying to stick apples on a tree with Sellotape®, rather than have the patience to allow the fruit to grow itself – in its *own way*.

And so often when we try to portray Christianity to our children, we are so keen for them to grasp it – to get them to share the faith we have – that we don't realize we are doing it in a way that may be comfortable for us, but is totally alien to them.

I think now of a father who wanted to show his son, Daniel, how to share his faith and decided to demonstrate this on two of the friends that the boy had invited home after school. Daniel had just wanted to die on the spot. Later, during an interlude in a PlayStation game, one of his friends said, "Your dad is very religious," and Daniel heard himself say, "Yeah – he's weird." And then he felt ashamed because he felt not only that he was betraying his father, but that he was actually betraying God. He never brought friends to the house again.

What a contrast that is with the experience of Sally, a girl I know who loves to bring her non-Christian friends home because she knows her mother will give them a genuine welcome and show a real interest in their lives. Her mother will make them laugh, and listen to their woes, and once in a while she will say something about her faith – but it will seem so natural. In fact, although Sally's family normally say grace before meals, they don't always do so when her non-Christian friends are at the table. Her mother wants to make people feel at home around that table – not awkward – and show that they are welcome and loved. Sally's mother believes that God understands that.

So, if God has no grandchildren, how do our children find faith for themselves as sons or daughters of God? It has been suggested that there are four distinct stages of faith in a child. Let's take a moment to look at them.

Experienced faith

Experienced faith is the first exposure to Christianity that children have. For the children of Christian parents it is usually because they are taught about the faith: Bible stories are read to them; prayers are said with them; they are told what does and does not please God; they are taken to church.

Experienced faith tells a child what is "normal" as a Christian. It could be worshipping loudly or being quiet in church. The fascinating thing about experienced faith is that later in life it will inform that child's theology. If, as a child, they see God portrayed at home and in church as someone who is quickly angered, that will often be their view of God in later life. If they observe a family or church that is accepting and loving, their picture of God will be like that.

If you want any proof of this, ask some of your Christian friends if they believe that God is pleased with them. Even though they may be feeding the poor, visiting the sick, preaching the word, and turning their neighbourhood upside down for Jesus, many will say, "No – I fail him a lot." They constantly feel unworthy – and therefore actually *unloved* by God. And often the reason is that the abiding image they have of God from childhood is his preoccupation with their sin.

Because this image of God is so prevalent for many Christians, one church leader I know regularly takes his church through a "What We Believe" basics course. And the first lesson is the most important. He says, "Our starting point is not the depravity of men and women, but the love of God." This is a church that teaches holy living. It doesn't ignore God's commands on how we should live, but its foundational belief – which it imparts to all its members from the children to the elderly – is that "God loves you".

The stage of experienced faith is a vital one. And the wonderfully encouraging – and totally frightening – fact is that at this stage *everything is formative*. The way children see us behave towards each other, the Bible messages they hear, how we deal with the "naughty" kids in their Sunday school class, what we say about giving to the poor – it is all formative. *Nothing* is lost.

Affiliative faith

This stage has some similarities with experienced faith in that the child's faith involves copying what he or she sees in those around them; they will join in because "everybody else does it".

If your children are young, take every opportunity to influence them for good. Take time to pass on your values, tell them what you believe, and demonstrate how you think life should be lived. Don't miss one second of that opportunity for the simple reason that, when they are small, your kids think that you know everything and have done everything worth doing. At that time of their lives, nobody on the face of the earth influences them more than you do. This opportunity is precious because the day is hurtling towards you when they may well think you are totally stupid and have done little worth doing, and they will be influenced more by other people.

You may well ask, "When will that happen?" and "Who will influence them?" It will happen the day your child becomes a teenager, and those who will influence them will be their peer group. These people, who in playgroups, nursery and junior school were no more than little friends, will suddenly grow into beings that for six or seven years will influence your child's life even more strongly than you.

It's a scary moment for parents when they realize that the child who has always looked to them for wisdom, guidance, and approval now thinks that Kylie Harrison, aged fourteen, is the cleverest human being on the planet, and would do anything to earn her praise. This is a time when parents hope that all the work they have put in during the pre-teen years is going to bear some fruit. And it better had, because, for a few years at least, many become helpless spectators of their children's lives.

So what does a parent who cares deeply about their child's spiritual and moral development do? First, don't give up totally during the "spectator" phase. You still have at least *some* influence. Even if your children seem to ignore your advice, they will often come back to it later on.

For most parents, there will come the challenge of "I don't want to go to church any more!" How we react to that statement, of course, depends on the age and emotional maturity of our child. But it's a difficult one. On the one hand, we know the dangers of "forcing" them to go to church and imagine them, aged fifty, saying, "They made me go as a child, but as soon as I could make my own mind up I didn't darken the door of a church again." On the other hand, there is a danger that we give up too easily and inadvertently deny our child a longer opportunity to be touched by the life of the local church – and maybe even to meet a friend or a mentor whom God will use to change their lives for ever.

Every parent needs a little help during this stage, and so, second, it's worth putting some real effort into helping your child find a peer group that will help to strengthen them in their faith and values. One way of doing this is to make sure that he or she is in a church youth group where the leader genuinely cares for them, and that that youth group is a really good one. This humble organization, which is often the butt of criticism from parents, is so important that I have dedicated Chapter Four to it.

Searching faith

This stage in a child's faith involves him or her asking questions and trying to understand the things they've already been taught. It is typically linked to the teenage years, although some youth leaders have told me they are seeing it happening with much younger children. One said, "It's very possible to have an earnest discussion with a ten-year-old about heaven and hell, the resurrection, and evolution."

It can be a scary stage for parents for three reasons. First, parents sometimes feel afraid that their children are beginning to doubt their faith, but this is not necessarily a bad thing. Most mature Christians who are honest will tell you that they still go through periods of doubt about various aspects of their faith – in fact, some would say it is almost impossible to develop a mature faith unless you do.

We all know that the most famous doubter in the Bible is Thomas, but perhaps the person who gives us the best example of how to deal with doubt is John the Baptist. He has been proclaiming Jesus as "the Lamb of God, who takes away the sin of the world".[2] He has been telling people that the Messiah has come. Then, suddenly, he is imprisoned by Herod and as he lies in his cell he begins to doubt.

But he decides to take those doubts to Jesus. He asks his disciples to go and ask the master, "Are you the one who was to come, or should we expect someone else?"[3] In other words, "Have I got it all wrong?" Jesus answers his doubts and then says, "There is no one greater than John."[4] John's doubts were not a problem to Jesus, and our children's doubts needn't be a problem to us.

Of course, the second reason we worry about our children having doubts is that we are afraid we won't be able to answer them. I believe that in the Christian community we sometimes have too many answers. When I was young I would have been able to tell you why God allows suffering (as I remember it, it was something to do with free will), but, to be honest, I couldn't give you an answer now. When our kids ask questions we should try our best to give them answers – and not be too proud to go to others for help. But if that's not possible there is nothing wrong in saying "I'm sorry, I just don't know". Encourage your children to be diligent in seeking answers to their doubts, but let them know that, this side of heaven, we simply will not know them all. Encourage them to bring their doubts to Jesus.

And, lastly, perhaps we are afraid of acknowledging our children's doubts because they remind us of our own. One mature Christian man told me that when he was a child he would listen as his father preached with tremendous certainty from the pulpit. Then he said, "But in the four walls of our home, Dad told me he had lots of doubts – he just couldn't air them in public."

Of course, it's not always appropriate to share our doubts – I have some sympathy for the atheist who said to the Christian, "Tell me your certainties – I have enough doubts of my own!" But what is certainly wrong is an atmosphere in church and at home that condemns questioning – searching – and gives the impression that the only faith worth having is one with no doubts.

I remember telling my kids not to get too excited when they read headlines in the newspapers such as "Archaeology Proves Bible True!" I would encourage them to read the articles, but also warn them that in a few months' time they might see headlines screaming,

"Archaeology Debunks Bible Myths!" I would urge them not to let their faith go up or down based on the prevailing winds.

Owned faith

This is when a child passes through the searching stage and is convinced that what they believe is true. Another way of putting it is that "they believe it for themselves". They may still have doubts and questions, but they will try to work through these. They may not fit the mould of other kids at your church, but nevertheless they are seeking to honour God: they have become disciples of Jesus.

The objective for any Christian parent is to help our children get to the place where they "own" their faith. Some kids come to that place at the age of twelve, others at thirty. But, ultimately, faith they don't own themselves won't survive.

God has no grandchildren.

Chapter 2

Avoid the Jelly-Mould Syndrome

D o you remember the title of the talk I mentioned in the first chapter – "How to Bring up Godly Children"? It may as well have been "How to Invest in the Stock Market Without Risk". You simply can't do it. We may think it *ought* to be possible, but it's not. And if we do believe that we can shoehorn our children into faith, we run the terrible risk of running up against the *jelly-mould syndrome*.

I don't know how effective your computer's spam filter is, but imagine you open your email one day and discover that the inbox is full of the stuff. You glance at the titles and then suddenly, in the middle of all the offerings that promise to make various bits of your body bigger or smaller or disappear completely, you see this: "Mould for the Perfect Christian Child."

Your son is nine and is beginning to drive you crazy… no, hang on a minute… has driven you crazy ever since the pregnancy test kit showed positive. You also remember that your mother used to have jelly moulds – some in the shape of rabbits, cats, cars and, in a nod to a more modern world, the starship *Enterprise*. You have seen how effective these things are: you take run-of-the-mill jelly that's sloshing about in a saucepan, pour it into the mould and, after it's set, end up with exactly the shape you want.

You can't resist! You open the email and read: "Get the kid of your dreams. Send now for our Christian Child Mould." It goes on: "Get a church-attending, sensible-dressing, worship-song-loving, youth-Bible-study-never-missing, rap-hating, tattoo-proofed, sermon-note-taking son or daughter. Full refund if child found smoking behind the church hall."

Let me tell you, there's hardly a parent on the face of the earth who wouldn't at least have been tempted to give it a try. Dianne and I have two children and I can assure you that at certain stages in their lives I'd have ordered three moulds, just in case one of them broke in transit.

We may smile at this foolishness, but the truth is that many of us *do* buy a mould. Our particular Christian tradition tells us what a good Christian child should look like and we spend a fair amount of our parenting effort trying to get our child to fit it. The only problem is that the mould doesn't seem to work too well. Well, that's not completely true; perhaps with one of our children it worked like a dream – for a while. But with our other children the jelly just ends up all over the floor. No matter how much we pull, yank, cajole and pray we simply cannot get this child to fit the mould. At times it seems to be working. We get them attending church and the youth Bible study – and then one day they walk in with a tattoo. Or we get them studying the Bible every day – and then find a cigarette butt under their daily reading notes.

Even then we continue to devote ourselves to making our child fit the mould. But one day he says to himself: "I can't do this any more. I'm not like the other kids at church. I love heavy metal music and I want to wear Goth clothes like my mates. And I can't stand all that singing on a Sunday. So I'm not a good Christian. I know Mum and Dad are disappointed with me and I probably embarrass them in front of their friends at church. I'm probably a disappointment to God as well. I've got to get out of this mould."

And our child does get out of it. In fact, he turns his

back on everything to do with faith because he feels such a failure at it all. And to your dying day you pray that one day he will eventually fit the mould. But you never see that moment. And when, finally, you get to heaven, you ask God why he never answered your prayers that your child turn out as you wanted.

He is tender with you for he knows the frailty of our hearts, and says, "Let me show you something." He takes your hand and leads you to a workshop. Above a small door is a sign: "Moulds for Christian Kids." And as you go through the door you gasp, for it opens out into a vast area and you see thousands, no millions, of moulds stretching into the distance.

The Father sees your face and says, "You look surprised." Eventually you find your tongue and say, "But there are so many – and they are all different!" He frowns and says, "Look closer." And as you do, you gasp again and stutter, "They are all different and yet, in some ways, *all the same.*"

"You have seen correctly," he says. "Every mould is different because every child is different, and yet all are the same because these are *my* moulds and I base every one of them on *my* Son. The plan all along was that they be like *him.*"

I sat recently with a young man in his twenties who

told me of the day when he was sixteen that he decided he couldn't go to church any more. It was because he was too ashamed of some of the things he did; smoking was one of them. He said, "I knew I didn't fit."

I know this boy. He has a heart for the poor; he would give his last pound – and he has never had many of those – to somebody in need. And, as I think of him, I wonder if somewhere in heaven there is a mould with his name on it that is shaped just like Jesus. In many of the things that really matter he was already beginning to fill that mould. But to this day he believes that God is displeased with him because he's never managed to fit the mould of a particular local church.

Some of that young man's contemporaries never left the church. In fact they fitted the mould perfectly. Some of them may go on to hold positions of responsibility in that most religious of establishments. But unlike him they may never care for the poor or have a heart for the disadvantaged. In fact, they may gossip, criticize and bully their way through local church life. It is true that they will rarely miss a church meeting, a daily quiet time or a chance to protest at the evils they see all around them. The only problem is that, unlike him, they will never feel ashamed.

You don't read much about Jesus getting angry, but,

when you do, you know that someone has really offended the very heart of his Father. One such incident is Jesus' withering condemnation of some of the religious leaders of his time who, with their endless rules and regulations, made ordinary people feel that they were failures before God. He said, "You put burdens on their shoulders that they just can't bear."

Allow me to paraphrase that: "You are trying to force them into a mould of your own making that they just can't fit." Unless we understand this we will continually be judging our children using the wrong criteria, and, in doing so, making some kids who really care about the things that matter to God feel second-class. It's a tragedy when a young person walks away from God because they don't want to be like Jesus. But it is a scandal when they feel they have to leave because, although they love him, they just can't be like *us*.

Lots of fifteen-year-old boys don't like sitting still. And they don't like singing. And they don't like reading. And they don't like listening to lectures. (The truth is that with regard to communication they live in a different world from us – which is why we simply cannot understand their ability to do their homework, listen to music and text their friends all at the same time.) And then they come to Christ. And we ask them to come to church and sit still, sing songs, read and listen to lectures. And after a while they stop coming to church. So we call them prodigals. Actually they aren't.

They just can't sit still.

Chapter 3

Don't Sweat the Small Stuff

I recently spoke with David, a man in his early twenties. He used to go to a church near where we live. I remember visiting it and seeing him in the worship band, hammering away at a keyboard and singing "Shine Jesus Shine" for all he was worth. I asked him why he didn't go to church any more. He sighed and said, "I stopped when I was seventeen. I became too ashamed to go, you know – because of what I'd started doing outside church."

I thought I knew both him and his family pretty well and I'd heard of no great scandals; perhaps that's what gave me the courage (or the foolishness) to ask: "What kind of things were you doing?"

He said, "I started running around with a really bad crowd. And I got my bottom lip pierced."

I haven't been able to get David out of my mind.

A friend of mine who is a politician was once asked to visit a new prison. It housed over three hundred men, and the tour took almost three hours. When it finished the governor invited him to his office and my friend asked, "How is the prison performing?"

The governor looked pleased with the question. "Exceptionally well," he said. "We are hitting over ninety-seven per cent of our forty-six key performance indicators."

"That's impressive," said my friend. "What kind of things do you measure?"

The governor frowned. "Well, the usual stuff. Health and safety, for example – every guard has to learn how to lift a prisoner who is injured. And then there's food and hygiene – every one of our meals has to pass a rigorous test set by our nutritionist and the soap containers must be kept topped up in all the cells."

"Do you measure reoffending rates?" my friend asked.

"I beg your pardon?" said the governor.

"I mean," my friend explained, "after they've finished their sentence, do you measure how many of the prisoners reoffend within a certain period? You know – to assess how successful you've been in helping them find a different way to live?"

"No, we don't do that," said the governor.

Isn't that strange? One of the single most important indicators of whether a prison has been successful or not is never measured.

Every church has a list of key performance indicators that allow its leaders and members to assess how its young people are doing. They may not be written down, but they are always there.

The young man I met recently, David, had been attending a good church, but somehow it had managed to convey to him that he was failing the test. The simple truth is that the more restrictive the questions, the easier it is to fail.

If, to be a good Christian girl, you have to attend church at least once a week, go to the youth Bible study, not wear more than the lightest touch of make-up, and not listen to heavy rock music, then even if you never miss a Sunday service you can still end up with a mark of just 25 per cent because you find the youth Bible study boring, you wear half an inch of make-up, and you're a Green Day fan. The only problem is – just like the prison governor – your church is measuring the wrong things.

So how can we choose the right things to measure? It's not easy, but fortunately we've been given a little help.

Jesus has told us some of the indicators he is going to use when we stand before him at the end of time. The passage in Matthew 25 is very clear: he will want to know whether we have fed the hungry, clothed the naked, visited the prisoners, cared for the sick and welcomed the stranger.[1] These are the equivalent of the "How many prisoners reoffend?" question. In heaven's eyes these are, at least, some of the big issues.

But because David's church had a list of "performance indicators" that were nowhere near what was high on God's agenda, all he heard were negative comments.

Most of us parent and manage people by catching them doing something wrong and criticizing them for it. This is how the Pharisees of Jesus' time handled people. And yet an opposite approach is almost always more productive. One of the most effective ideas I have ever discovered as a parent and as an employer is to catch people doing something *right* – and praise them for it. It is an absolutely vital principle, because when the ear never hears praise, the heart loses the will to try.

Let's look at how the principle of "catch them doing something *right*" might have worked in this local church. Rewind the clock and imagine David is seventeen again. He is still playing in the worship band and it is true there are still things he needs to deal with – being a little wiser about the friends he chooses, for one. Both his parents and his youth leader hope that there won't be any more ironmongery inserted into various bits of his body and, yes, they are still trying to encourage him to go to the youth Bible study.

But, despite this, he knows that on some of the big issues – some of the ones that really matter to God and therefore the ones this church emphasizes – he is, with God's help, at least making some progress. He always uses some of the money from his evening job to buy a copy of the *Big Issue* from the homeless guy who stands outside Starbucks; when one of the kids from school was in a motorbike accident he was one of the first to visit him in hospital; and next month he will be running a half-marathon to raise money for a hospital in Uganda.

The practical outworking of "catch them doing something *right*" is that, instead of David feeling too ashamed to go to church because of its concern over some minor issues, the church leader asks whether he'd mind being interviewed in the Sunday service about the forthcoming marathon and what he hopes to achieve for the African hospital.

As I consider that scenario, two words come to mind. The first is *belonging* : I have no doubt that in this situation David would have felt part of the church. And the second is *valued*: he would have felt valued for the way he was trying to serve God, instead of condemned for missing some tick boxes on the "perfect Christian child" hit list. It's easy to criticize young people, but the truth is that many teenagers have commendable qualities and attitudes that put some older people to shame: they care about the environment more than we did; they are less racist than we were; they care about the poor and social justice more than we did.

Let's imagine how it might have been different for David. It wouldn't have been hard to find at least *something* with which to encourage him. He was a young man with a good heart. That's not to say there weren't important problem areas in his life that needed to be addressed – but that's true in the life of every Christian. It *could* have been different.

But for David it's too late.

A couple of years ago, while speaking to church leaders in North Carolina, USA, I met a pastor who told me a wonderful story. A young man had tried to enter their church on a Sunday morning. He looked like something out of a sixties movie: long hair, torn jeans and – the real problem – no shoes. In any event, he didn't get far. A middle-aged man approached him and said, "I'm sorry, but you can't come into this church with no shoes on – this is God's house."

The young man didn't protest, just turned quietly away and made for the door. And then he felt a tug at his sleeve. A very elderly man stood there – one of the founders of the church – and he said to him, "Please don't go!" And with that the old man sat in a pew and bent to untie his laces with arthritic fingers, took off his shoes and socks, and pushed them under the pew in front. Then he looked up at the deacon who had tried to keep the younger man out and said, "It's alright – he can sit by me."

When my son Lloyd was sixteen he started smoking. I remember one day when he was sitting beside me in church and I could smell the smoke on his clothes. I thought to myself, "If I can smell it, so can the people around us. I'm the chairman of Care for the Family… I write books on parenting… I need this like a hole in the head."

And then I stopped myself going further down that line of thought. I reached across and put my arm around Lloyd and said, "Son, it's great to have you in church with me today." Did I want him to stop smoking? Yes. Was I glad when he did? Of course. But I wasn't going to make my son feel an outcast in church over something like that. Jesus said to the religious leaders of his time, "Woe to you, teachers of the law and Pharisees, you hypocrites! You give a tenth of your spices – mint, dill and cummin. But you have neglected the more important matters of the law – justice, mercy and faithfulness."[2] It is the duty of every generation of believers to ask God, "What really matters to you?" Perhaps we will have to be prepared to lay down our lives for those things. But don't make somebody feel a rebel over things that are not high on God's agenda. Don't drive them from church and into the arms of the enemy over secondary issues. Don't make them ashamed over things that heaven does not find shameful.

Don't sweat the small stuff.

Chapter 4

Create a Sense of Belonging

When we considered the topic of experienced faith a few chapters ago, I spoke of the crucial need for our children to be part of a youth group where the leader genuinely cares for them and which is a really good one.

You'll notice that I put the bit about finding a caring youth leader first. That's because it is possible for your child to thrive in a youth group that has just five people, primitive facilities, and an annual treat consisting of a trip to the nearest town for fish and chips – so long as the leader *really* cares and the kids know that they are special to him or her. It doesn't matter much whether the leader is twenty or fifty, is cool or dresses in tweed. The crucial thing is that the kids sense they are loved.

The man who changed my life died just a few years

ago. Arthur was almost eighty; I remember visiting him in hospital, sitting by his bed while he was asleep and allowing my mind to go back over the years.

I first met him as I walked down a street near my home. I was in my mid-teens and life was not exactly humming. School seemed like a foreign country from which I was about to be deported. My teacher had written in my report, "He is making no use of what little ability he has." My parents didn't go to church but I'd gone to the Sunday school at the end of our road since I was small, although I was about to drop out of that. My twin ambitions were to become a rock and roll singer and to snog Carol Pearce. (I achieved one of them – and then only briefly.)

When we met in the street that day, Arthur told me that he was starting a Bible course at his home and asked if I'd like to come. If your main dream is to perform at sell-out concerts and have girls throw articles of clothing at you, a Bible study on a Wednesday night isn't the greatest offer you've ever had. But for some reason I said yes.

In some ways Arthur had little going for him in the home-study arena. First, he had never passed an academic examination and he had little grasp of theology. Second, he was a dreadful communicator; he often got his words horribly mangled. And the home where we had the study wasn't exactly palatial; Arthur and his wife, Margaret, were poor – they had just two small rooms in a shared house.

But they had something that made up for all this. They loved kids – especially ones that didn't fit in to church too easily. They loved us by not boring us for longer than twenty-five minutes with the Bible study, and by using some of the little money they had to buy us fish and chips afterwards. And they loved us by setting up a table-tennis table made out of two bits of hardboard. (There was only a foot of space at either end – if the ball went under the table we had to perform an engineering job to retrieve it.) And they loved us by hunting us down if we ever missed a week. But, most of all, they made us feel special. No matter what teachers said about you, when you walked into Arthur's home, you felt like a king.

When I was seventeen he told me that he thought God had given me a gift of public speaking. I told him to forget it – I wasn't the kind of child even to put my hand up in class. Arthur said I didn't have a choice in the matter: if God had given me a gift then I was stuck with it – and he was going to help me develop it. This was not an encouraging prospect – Arthur wasn't exactly the most skilled orator you'd ever met.

But teach me he did, and made me practise in his "best room", with my notes perched on the mantelpiece. And one day he told me I was ready to face my public: at first talking to children and later to adults as I "gave my testimony".

In the years since then I have spoken to many people across the world. On one occasion I had been invited to address a conference attended by over a thousand lawyers. Just before it started I called Arthur and said, "You taught me to do this. Thank you."

He laughed and said, "Did I?" Some time ago I was being interviewed on a radio station in America and they rang Arthur at his home as a surprise for me. The presenter asked him what he now thought of the boy who used to come to his Bible class. He said, "I'm proud of him." I cried on air.

Arthur taught me so much. He taught me that you don't have to have great talent to be used by God – you just have to be prepared to use what you do have. He taught me that if you can't do something yourself, then you can still help somebody else do it – and so touch people you may never see. He taught me that you don't have to be young to be a great youth worker. But, above all, Arthur and Margaret taught me that the greatest gifts we can give our kids are love and acceptance.

During the pre-teen and teenage years children will usually want to feel they belong to and are accepted by their peer group. Typical church activities such as car washing to raise money for charities, going to hear Christian bands, camps, and youth club all give them the chance to deepen their relationships with other Christians their own age and are vital as affiliative faith deepens.

And yet, in spite of their importance in our children's lives, it's easy to take the youth group and the youth leader for granted. If we are wise we won't do that. We'll be careful not to clog up our kids' lives with piano lessons, judo, maths tutoring and ballet classes to the point where they just don't have time to spend with kids their own age from church. Instead, everybody in our family will know that Friday night is youth-club night.

It's easy to get it wrong in this area because we say to ourselves, "Well, the kids are in church on a Sunday. What does it matter if they're not part of the youth group?" The truth is, they probably go to church to please you and will stop when it becomes too big a price to pay. But, generally, kids *want* to go to a good youth group – and, even if they don't, that will change when they find just *one* friend there that they click with. Pray with all your heart for that friend to show up.

Take this seriously. Get to know your kids' youth leaders and encourage them whenever you can. Be careful not to develop a "ministry of discouragement" – telling the leaders when they've got it right is normally much more effective than carping criticism. Of course, tell them when you're worried. Most youth leaders are savvy enough to be able to take your genuine concerns for your children on board, while not getting too agitated by your parental desire to make life perfect for your offspring: "He likes computer games best"; "She needs plenty of encouragement."

Church youth work is vital in our children's lives, so why then is it so often a battleground between parents and youth leaders? Whenever I hear that churches are going through what is euphemistically described as "a difficult time", my mind always goes to the three big issues about which churches regularly fight. It matters not whether the church is based in Putney or Portugal, Guatemala or Gretna Green; these three issues rarely change, and they are: the building, the style of worship, and the youth work.

Disputes over whether to go ahead with a million-pound building project when there's only five hundred pounds in the bank I can understand. Arguments over whether to raise the roof in worship or sit meditating I can comprehend. But why so many rows over the *youth work*? I have a theory: youth leaders are permissible targets for every parent who is disappointed that the leaders have not been able to put right in one night a week what the parents themselves have not been able to put right in fifteen years of their child's life.

The parents may never have studied the Bible with their children, but they want the youth leader to turn little Justin into a theologian. Mum and Dad may have ducked the issues of sex, drugs and rock 'n' roll, but they fully expect the youth leader to draw diagrams of genitalia and cannabis plants, and warn their kids of the evils of bands like Lostprophets.

And, often, parents are so concerned for the spiritual welfare of their children that they totally misunderstand the value of the so-called "non-spiritual" side of youth work. Perhaps they give the youth leader a hard time because "there's not enough Bible study in the group" or "the young people should be praying together more".

I understand those concerns, but often parents miss the value of what they so easily write off as "the social stuff" – the trips to the ice rink, the barbeques, the sponsored walks and the all-night computer-games marathon. Don't despise these humble activities; they can have an incredible influence for spiritual good in the life of your child. When your son or daughter is having a good time with people who love God, you make it a little easier for him or her to feel they "belong" to that community.

While we're talking about creating a sense of belonging, let me share a tip a youth leader gave me: "Make your place the place to hang out." You may not live in a massive house, but if you can serve coffee and dish out a few biscuits (or, in respect of teenage boys, a few *packets* of biscuits!), that's all that's needed. When you accept your children's friends, you also make your children feel accepted. Try to share this out between other parents and their homes. It all feeds affiliative faith. The child learns, "These are my roots"; "These are my people."

To deliver on the need to find a good youth group should be the waking thought of every parent of teenagers. And if your church hasn't got one, then either start one or find a church that has – there are worse reasons for leaving a church than trying to find one with a good youth ministry that your kids want to be part of.

I'm not talking about trying to find the *perfect* youth group: just a bunch of kids who can hang out together, laugh together, and occasionally cry together; where those a little further on in their faith can encourage those who are struggling. In short, a place where your children feel they *belong*.

Problems arise for kids when they have very few opportunities for affiliative faith. Perhaps there are no, or hardly any, young people in their church. In this situation they can easily feel there's nobody they gel with. They begin to say to themselves, "I just don't fit in here." I believe it is vital for both parents and churches to take this seriously and to move heaven and earth to help young people get those experiences of affiliation. That could be done by linking up with youth groups from a larger church, getting involved in organizations such as Urban Saints, Youth for Christ and The Message, or attending events such as Soul Survivor, New Wine, Keswick or Spring Harvest.

What we are considering here is not marginal. Whether or not your child finds a group of friends they feel comfortable with in your faith community will be one of the most significant factors (perhaps *the* most significant) in determining their attitude to church and their desire to keep going in their faith.

I honestly wonder whether there's anybody on the face of the earth who is less enthusiastic about "church hopping" than I am. I believe that whenever possible we should persevere in our local church. Nevertheless, if your local church has little to help your child build strong relationships with his or her peer group – and so build this sense of affiliative faith – perhaps, as I've already said, you really should consider moving church for their sake.

Just don't leave it too late.

I remember an African friend telling me about "the Big Five". These are the animals that any visitor to one of the great national parks of Africa hopes to see: lion, elephant, cheetah, buffalo, and rhino. But of course in these parks the animals live as if in the wild, and there is many a tourist who has discovered that, actually, one of the Big Five is looking for him.

The Big Five also stalk through our homes and churches. The next five chapters deal with them: Over-busyness; Cynicism; Hypocrisy; Judgmentalism; and Overfamiliarity. In their ability to bring harm to, and even kill, the faith of our children, they are at least as efficient as the five that stalk the national parks in Africa...

Chapter 5

Over-busyness

Dianne was holding a seminar at Spring Harvest (a major Christian festival in the United Kingdom) for the partners of church leaders. There was a question-and-answer session and, as it invariably does, the discussion turned to the special pressures that they so often feel. As Dianne cast her eyes around the room she noticed a young girl of perhaps twelve with her hand up at the back. Dianne gestured for the girl to ask her question. She says she will never forget that child's voice echoing across the room and the words that she spoke: "I know that my father is doing God's work, but can somebody tell me why I never see him?"

Of course it's not just children who are affected by over-busyness. Some years ago I received an anonymous letter from a church leader's wife. It contained a poem. It moved me because I have no doubt that this woman loved her husband and that he had no idea what his busy life was doing to their relationship.

I want my husband to smile again.

I want to be able to talk to him after dinner.

I want our family to go out on Saturdays for a walk or a shopping trip.

I want to be me – not "the minister's wife".

I want to sit in church, listen to the notices, and decide what *I would like to go to*.

I want my husband to come home at night and relax instead of just recharging the batteries and disappearing out again.

I want to celebrate birthdays and anniversaries always, not just when there are no church meetings.

I want to be able to tell the self-centred and self-righteous folk that they are.

I want him to come in at night and talk to us instead of slumping silently, reliving the awkward visit or difficult meeting he's been at.

I want people to stop telling me how wonderful it must be to be the minister's wife and then complain they've not had a visit for months.

I want people who regularly miss meetings because they've "had a busy day" to let us miss occasional meetings because we've "had a busy day".

I want him to come with me sometimes to see our

child swim or play football.

I want him to be my husband instead of their minister.

And I want not to be guilty about these things.

At the bottom of the poem is a PS: "Tonight is one of those nights when it is all too much for me. I hope that you will read this and maybe pray for us even though you don't know us."

I sometimes think about this woman who wrote to a stranger with such a cry from the heart and I wonder whether life is better now for her and her child.

But what of the question the young girl asked at Spring Harvest? In truth it was never answered. How could it be? Only her father could explain why he worked such long hours in the church, why he said yes to just about everybody who asked him to do anything, and why his daughter felt like an orphan – perhaps even resenting God for "robbing" her of her father.

Over the years I have had many conversations with Christians about being over-busy in the local church, often to the detriment of their own families. Sometimes they have pointed out to me that Jesus said we must put him before our family. But that cannot mean that, in an effort to serve others, we neglect those for whom we have *primary* responsibility.

Of course some families have had to endure separation for the sake of serving Christ, but that is quite different from a child feeling of little value simply because a mother or father cannot say no to anybody. Jesus did not live his life in furious busyness. Instead, he had an incredible sense of what God wanted him to do. And because he knew what he was meant to be saying yes to, he had the freedom also to say no. "Will you be our king?" – "No."[1] "Will you settle this dispute between my brother and me?" – "No."[2] On another occasion the crowds asked him to stay with them, but he said, "No, we are going on."[3]

There is a very scary verse for over-busy people in the book of Ecclesiastes: "...all labour and all achievement spring from man's envy of his neighbour."[4] In other words, what so often drives us into what seems to be the selfless service of others may actually be the need to prove ourselves to somebody else. Our lack of security propels us into lives of furious activity in which we strive to demonstrate our worth. The strange thing about this is that so often it affects men and women who, at least in the eyes of others, have nothing to prove at all. There is little peace for such a man or woman. Henri Nouwen put it like this:

Whilst complaining about too many demands, I felt uneasy when none were made. Whilst speaking about the burden of letter writing, an empty mailbox made me sad. Whilst fretting about giving lecture tours, I felt disappointed when there were no invitations. Whilst speaking nostalgically about an empty desk, I feared the day when that would come true.

In short, whilst desiring to be alone, I was frightened of being left alone.[5]

When we are pursued by the demon of busyness, there is no end to the things we feel "must be done". But so often when we are doing these we miss the *main* thing, and there is nothing more useless than doing effectively that which should never be done at all.

I have made some bad mistakes in this area. For fifteen years I was heavily involved in church leadership as well as holding down a nine-to-five job. There were always meetings to attend, sermons to prepare, and phone calls that always came just as I had just started playing with the kids or reading them a bedtime story. I think I almost lost my family because of my foolish over-busyness. But, perhaps even worse than that, I ran the risk of alienating them from the very God I was trying to serve – because, very simply, although I loved my family and would have given my life for them, I was not *demonstrating* that love. Love needs time.

One young man said to me, "When I was a kid, my dad was always so busy in the church. Every Monday night he had an elders' meeting. I remember thinking, 'What's so important at church that they have to meet *every* Monday?' "

I think I can answer that boy's question: "Nothing was so important. They just got into the habit of it."

When I was involved in church leadership we used to meet every Monday as well – often until after midnight. Then one day I realized that we were spending hours discussing things that could easily have been dealt with more efficiently. And so I said, "From now on, I'm going to leave these meetings at ten o'clock – and it's for this reason: if what we're discussing isn't important, it can wait until next time. And if it *is* important, then what on earth are we doing discussing it when we're all shattered?"

From the looks on the other leaders' faces the first time I left that meeting early, I gathered that the world might be about to end. But soon we were all leaving at ten. And, to this day, nobody can quite remember what we used to talk about in those midnight sessions.

I remember asking Dr R. T. Kendall, former senior

minister of Westminster Chapel, one of the most famous churches in the UK, what one thing he would change if he could turn the clock back. He answered in a heartbeat: "I would put my children before the church. It would make me a better father – and a better minister."

It is not always possible to give your children all the time you would want, but if you really want to get them through church without them ending up hating God, make sure they don't see the church as the main competitor for your time – and love.

Chapter 6

Cynicism

We turn now to one of the most efficient killers among the Big Five – perhaps not the most dangerous, but a potent destroyer of the seed of faith in the hearts of our children. It is so effective because it slowly chokes the ability to believe, to see God at work, and to experience the reality of his love and presence. Let's see how it operates.

It is 1.30 pm and you and your family have just sat down to Sunday lunch. As you are carving the meat you say to your wife, "When that woman leads the worship she drives me crazy. By the time we'd sung that song five times I'd lost the will to live."

Your wife replies, "You were lucky you went out with the kids to their class before the sermon. It was like stand-up comedy. He told jokes and stories, and played us some Beatles music. The only thing we didn't get was any decent teaching. I just sat there and read my Bible – it wasn't worth listening to."

Remember what we said in an earlier chapter – "Every word counts. Every action is formative. *Nothing* is lost". And nothing is lost on your seven-year-old daughter and your ten-year-old son as they sit around that Sunday lunch table and listen to their parents. The message they get is that the leaders in their church are either ungodly or fools – or perhaps both. The seeds you sow that Sunday will grow and one day, aged fifteen, one of them will say, "I don't want to go there any more. The worship is rubbish and the sermons are lame." Don't expect that when they are fifteen you will be able to talk your way out of that and convince them otherwise.

And don't bring your youth leaders down in front of your children. If you think the youth leaders are stupid, naïve, inexperienced and irresponsible, then your kids will think the same – and maybe share their wisdom with the whole group. And if they think that, don't expect them to trust the youth leaders in anything – especially in matters of faith.

A friend of mine who has attended a large London church for many years told me a remarkable thing. He said that when his children were small he and his wife made a vow: it was that their children would never hear them speak negatively about their church. He said, "It was hard. Our church is a great place, but sometimes it drives me crazy. Sometimes we've had to hold our feelings in during the car journey home and keep our mouths shut over lunch, but I think I can say we have managed to keep our vow. Whenever possible we speak positively about what we have seen and heard." I asked him how he deals with things he's not happy with. He said, "My wife and I talk about it privately and if it's serious enough I go to the leaders. But I search my heart for things about which to be positive. I want my kids to see church through eyes that look for God at work."

Cynicism is different from criticism and we have to be careful not to simply squash our children's criticisms about church life. We have to learn to help them exercise their critical faculties in a way that does not lead to cynicism. If they come home complaining about church (and they will), that's a good time to get them to assess what's helpful about their criticism and what's not, and perhaps to help them see another perspective. Can we encourage them to explain to us how they feel, rather than interrogate them? Perhaps we can gently challenge their assumptions.

This is a chance for our kids to talk to us and to feel listened to. Don't despair when their criticism comes thick and fast: "Dad, I hate that speaker – he's boring." "Why do we have to stand and sing so much?" It's better for them to voice their criticism to us – and for us to try to bring a little balance – than for them to be too uninterested to be critical because they just don't care.

And be careful about labelling your child a cynic: you might encourage them – to some kids, "cynic" can be a pretty cool badge to wear.

Before we leave this potent killer of faith from the Big Five, let me say a little about cynicism with regard to expressions of church life that are different from our own. In other words: treating the wider Christian community with respect. You may be a card-carrying charismatic who tells your friends how boring you would find the worship in the local Brethren assembly, or you may be a staunch reformed Baptist who regularly holds forth on the shallowness of churches that "have no regard for biblical teaching and care only about experiences". That kind of talk is not very clever anyway, but voicing such views in front of our children is foolish in the extreme. And it's for this simple reason: if your children ever turn their back on God, you will be grateful for the day when they again start attending *any kind of church*.

My daughter, Katie, was a very easy child. She never wanted to go clubbing when she was sixteen and I never smelt alcohol on her breath when she was seventeen. And Katie never complained about attending church, youth groups, Spring Harvest – or anything at all. So I knew in my heart what would happen when she went to university. She would immediately join the Christian Union and then find a church near the campus and start attending. I rang up some contacts in the city where she would be living and Katie was invited to meals, Bible-study groups, and a zillion other things that would ensure that she stayed on the straight and narrow.

But the really scary thing for a parent about the compliant child is that, because all your attention has been on your other, more challenging offspring (trying to prevent them running off to South America with the girl they've just met at their Saturday job in Pizza Hut), you take them for granted. And after Katie had been at university for a few months it became apparent that, while not exactly letting her hair down, the "straight and narrow" wasn't top of her agenda. Apart from the odd occasion when she came home from uni, she stopped attending church completely.

That lasted for almost four years. By then she was working as a lawyer in London, and one day she rang Dianne and said, "Mum, I don't know what's happening, but I feel a deep need to start going to church again."

Dianne said, "I'll come up to London next weekend and we'll go together."

Katie had been brought up attending a small Brethren assembly at first and later an independent, "slightly charismatic" church in the middle of a vast housing estate. I asked Dianne where she was going to take Katie. When she told me, I thought to myself that our daughter was in for a bit of a culture shock.

The building in which this church meets is, by any standards, both beautiful and impressive. In fact quite different from the one Katie attended for most of her young life (which, although very practical, may well be one of the ugliest structures in Christendom!). And it has a wonderful orchestra that is, to say the least, a little more sophisticated than our "worship band" (hardly any tattoos at all on the bassoonists!). I could go on – just about everything was different from what Katie had known before. But I think it was partly that difference that touched her heart. Some may have found the worship not spontaneous enough, but Katie felt "safe" there. And the church welcomed her.

It was not the kind of church that Dianne and I were used to, but I thanked God that, although we had got lots wrong as parents, neither of us had ever sown in Katie's heart a cynical seed that said, "Other churches are rubbish – this is the only way to worship God."

Both Katie and her husband have been members of a

church for several years now that is much more like the one she attended when she was young. But Dianne and I have never lost the sense of debt we owe that London church, which, although so different from our own tradition, was used by God to touch our daughter's life.

Run from cynicism. It is corrosive – in our own hearts and in the lives of those we touch. There have been times in my life when I have been cynical and there have been times when I have been gullible. I don't want to be either, but to be honest, as I get older, I realize I would far rather be gullible than cynical – especially as a father.

I have learned that the voice of my cynicism will make it harder for my children to hear the voice of God.

Chapter 7

Hypocrisy

There's hardly a parent on earth who wouldn't at times consider running for cover when the issue of hypocrisy comes up. We know all too well that so often, when we're at home, we are not exactly the people we seem to be outside it. We've all heard funny stories of things that kids let out of the bag when the vicar happens to be visiting. It's just that most of us don't laugh: we know that next week it could be *our* kid and *our* vicar.

But don't immediately go on a guilt trip. One of the most vital tasks of any parent is to allow their children to see them fail. When our kids are young they think we are brighter than their teachers, prettier than their heroines and even holier than the vicar. But as they get older they see the cracks appear. And after they have realized that we are not the clever, handsome or holy people they used to believe we were, they also discover that some of the other stuff about us is not so attractive either.

They catch us being moody or wrongly angry over some minor issue. They hear some bad language or see a materialistic streak that doesn't suit a disciple of the carpenter too well. As we try to follow Christ we aim high for holiness, for compassion, for grace and love. And often we fail. At such times, it is very tempting to slip on a mask that makes others think we have attained those things – perhaps even to try to convince ourselves that we have. But it's not wise – or necessary.

At such times a child isn't helped by seeing his or her parents' failings covered up, but by seeing them being sorry for what they have done. Our children need to actually hear and watch us apologize to each other, to them and to others. It doesn't do an older child any harm to see his or her father or mother in tears because of the wrong they have done. This is about being honest, about modelling our own need for forgiveness from our family and from God.

But Jesus warned of a much deeper kind of hypocrisy and the incredible damage it could do. This kind of hypocrisy is a calculated, systematic, attempt to show yourself in a good light with no real effort or care to actually be the man or woman you are pretending to be. Eugene Peterson, author of *The Message*, puts it like this:

The Christian has more to fear from hypocrisy than anything else. Nothing stirred Jesus to hotter indignation. Jesus unfailingly approached the everyday sort of sinners who robbed, broke the Sabbath, engaged in prostitution, and even murdered, with inviting compassion. Hypocrites got nothing but His denunciation. The fiery passage in Matthew 23 seethes with anger as Jesus lets loose a string of "woes" against those who practice none of it, who spend enormous amounts of time tidying up the externals and ignore all the internal realities that count with God.[1]

Jesus said: "I've had it with you! You're hopeless, you religion scholars, you Pharisees! Frauds! Your lives are roadblocks to God's kingdom. You refuse to enter, and won't let anyone else in either."[2]

There's no getting away from the fact that, when it occurs in the home, hypocrisy of this kind can have an incredibly negative effect on our children's perception of what it means to be a follower of Jesus. Hypocrisy like this is making long prayers in public at church, whereas our children know we never pray in private. Hypocrisy is preaching messages on love, yet being cold to our wife and children. Hypocrisy gives thousands to the church building appeal – and lets others know – but walks past a needy person in the street without another thought. And hypocrisy like this is such a killer of faith in a child because it whispers that nothing is real – nothing is as it seems.

Research by the Barna group identified hypocrisy as one of the major reasons given by young people for turning away from God: "Young people reject Jesus because they feel rejected by Christians. We are responsible when our actions misrepresent God and push people away."[3]

Listen to the words of one young woman:

My dad was always wonderful to people in the church. He would smile and his face would light up whilst talking to them. But when we got home he would scream – literally scream – at me and my brother with rage. He would close the door to the vicarage quietly and then hurl his coat across the hall. Whatever we did was wrong. If we were too early for church he would shout at us that we hadn't shined our shoes properly. If we were late there would be hell to pay at the dinner table afterwards. If my mother tried to talk to him he would yell at her until she stopped sticking up for us. He broke her spirit. And because he was so different with people at church, nobody would ever believe what he was like at home. I don't think I rebelled in terms of what I believed. I just lost all confidence in myself or any sense of self worth.

When Spurgeon preached on the words of Jesus in Matthew chapter five about not hiding your light under a bushel, he asked his congregation to remember that the location of the lamp is the home. Spurgeon's point was clear: it is in the home that people really see who we are.

> ...the lamp should be seen by "all that are in
> the house", and so should the Christian's graces.
> Household piety is the best of piety. If our light is not
> seen in the house, depend upon it we have none...
> Lord, let me be zealous to spread abroad the light I
> have received from thee, even throughout the world!
> But at least let me shine in my own home.[4]

This is a call to be "real". We don't have to bounce about in worship if our hearts are breaking – we can let our children see our tears in the kitchen and later in church. We don't have to tell everybody on Sunday that we are well if our depression has reared its head again – we can let our children see us share our emotional hurt with trusted friends. But it also means that we can't just give or listen to sermons on forgiveness. We have to forgive each other in the home: our children for mistakenly erasing a week's work from our hard disk; our wife for the way she spoke during that row in the bedroom that the kids heard a mile away; and *ourselves* for the stupid way we get so screwed up over so little.

We don't have to be perfect. But imagine for a moment that we could at least pretend to be – and pull it off. Imagine that our children only ever saw the good side of us. Let your mind race with the possibility that we can send them into life with the belief that they can be like us – ever-praying, always-giving, never hassled, never rude, confident yet humble, attractive yet chaste, holy yet fun. Imagine that we ushered them into life believing that the mask was real and they could wear it for the rest of their lives. Imagine it: never failing, always achieving, in no need of support or counsel or forgiveness.

Imagine we loved them so little that we did that to them.

Chapter 8

Judgmentalism

When I was at school there were identical twins in my class. It really was the stuff of boys' comics. They would regularly fool the teachers: one would do detention for the other and in cross-country runs one would take over from his brother half way around the course and break the tape laughing. Everyone else in the class longed to have a twin. Hypocrisy, the issue we have just looked at, has a twin – its name is judgmentalism. You see them together so often. But, unlike the twins in my class, they are not identical. Judgmentalism sets the standards and hypocrisy says, "I have kept them." Hypocrisy loves the mask; judgmentalism loves the rules.

If Christianity is seen as a religion of rules and regulations, and if these rules are seen as our priorities, we will be judged by our own standards. And we will often be found wanting. When the Barna group, in a survey of Christian adults, asked what the most important thing was about being a Christian, the majority said: lifestyle – being good, doing the right thing, not sinning.[1] Of course all these are important, but it is sobering to see what other attributes were way down the list: discipleship, evangelism, worship, serving others and helping the poor.

In *unChristian*[2], David Kinnaman and Gabe Lyons discuss their in-depth research into why young adults in particular are disaffected with church in the USA. Their conclusion is that for many young people – perhaps *our* children – the public face of church appears, ironically, distinctly "unChristian"; and it is the issue of judgmental attitudes that is often the main cause of their disillusionment with the church. Jim White, a pastor, is quoted in the book. He says, "We fall prey to the charge of hypocrisy because we have reduced spirituality to a list of moral benchmarks coupled with a good dose of judgementalism."

Our children are likely to have far more difficulty with this issue than we did simply because society is now generally much more tolerant. Unless we do a good job in passing on our values effectively and demonstrating genuine love and care for those who do not share them, they will perceive us to be, at best, unfair and, at worst, bigoted.

David Kinnaman[3] put it like this:

I was surprised at how relentlessly Scripture warns believers *against being judgmental*. In addition to Jesus' cautionary words, the Bible makes it clear that God, not humans, should judge. It is God's job, and he does it impartially while exposing the true motives of people's hearts...

You've probably encountered believers who justify their own judgmental attitudes by reading you the first chapter of the book of Romans. This is the part of the Bible that describes God's anger "against all sinful, wicked people who push the truth away from themselves."[4]

...Yet Paul moves from his sharp discussion of sin to this wake up call for Christians: "You may be saying 'What terrible people you have been talking about!' But you are just as bad, and you have no excuse! When you say they are wicked and should be punished, you are condemning yourself, for you do these very same things... Don't you realize how kind, tolerant, and patient God is with you? Or don't you care? Can't you see how kind he has been in giving you time to turn from your sin?"[5]

Of course, so often we manage to hold both our judgmental spirit and our professed love for those who we think have fallen short in the same hand, but the result is not often convincing. Sophie, aged nineteen, put it like this: "Church people talk a lot about hating sin and loving sinners, but when you see how they act I sometimes think they hate the sin and the sinner."

David Kinnaman continues:

> Young people will understand that we believe certain
> lifestyles are wrong, but what they will not accept
> is an attitude that at times can only be described as
> "hate" towards those who do not comply. They are
> naturally more accepting than us, and if they believe
> that to follow Christ means adopting an adversarial
> stance towards those who have different views, they
> are quite likely to walk away from that. This is tragic
> because Jesus did the opposite to almost all groups –
> "almost" because he reserved his opposition for the
> religious who were hypocrites.[6]

But why is a judgmental example so very dangerous for the faith of our children? We touched on part of the answer a few chapters ago when we looked at the issue of "experienced faith" – one of the ways that our children grow in knowledge of God. Let me remind you what we said there: "The fascinating thing about experienced faith is that later in life it will inform that child's theology. If, as a child, they see God portrayed at home and in church as somebody who is quickly angered, that will often be their view of God in later life. If they observe a family or church that is accepting and loving, their picture of God will be like this."

In short, when our children observe a judgmental attitude in their church, and particularly in their parents, they develop a theology that believes that is God's attitude towards them. They run the risk not only of becoming judgmental themselves, but of coming to believe that God judges them in the same way that they have seen their parents judge others – quickly, decisively, and with little compassion. Such a child will run from God. I have begged church leaders not to say to their children, "You're a pastor's son. If you behave like this, what will people think of me?" And I urge them not to do so with these words: "If you say that to your children, then they will come to believe it is how God thinks of them. And it's not."

It may be that we are judgmental because we are playing to the wrong audience. Instead of trying to please God we are looking over our shoulder at what other Christians think of us. Instead of seeing people's potential as followers of Christ, we set ourselves up as spiritual judge and jury. The judgmental attitude is never attractive, rarely makes us want to stay, and can never make us feel that we are accepted – let alone loved.

Philip Yancey puts his finger on it:

Having spent time around "sinners" and also around purported saints, I have a hunch why Jesus spent so much time with the former group: I think he preferred their company. Because the sinners were honest about themselves and had no pretence, Jesus could deal with them. In contrast, the saints put on airs, judged him, and sought to catch him in a moral trap. In the end it was the saints, not the sinners, who arrested Jesus.[7]

What can we do as parents to help our children in this area? Perhaps the most important thing is to model a forgiving attitude to others. Jesus once gave an incredible tip to help us on the day when we have to face God ourselves. He said, "Do not judge, or you too will be judged. For in the same way as you judge others, you will be judged, and with the measure you use, it will be measured to you."[8] What an incredible incentive to say to those who have hurt us, "I forgive you. Forget it! No problem!"

Some time ago I met a woman after the service in our church one Sunday. She looked upset, so I asked if I could help her. She handed me a piece of paper and said, "I just found this note under the windscreen wiper on my car." I read it. It said, "Because of your inconsiderate parking you blocked me in and I am now late. Not a very Christian thing to do!"

A few weeks later at church it was my turn to preach; we were considering together the subject of judgmental attitudes. I told the story of the note on the car and said, "I don't know if the person who put that note there is a Christian or not, but if you are and you happen to be here today, let me say this to you. You had every right to put that note on the car of somebody who had done wrong to you and acted without care towards you. But you should know this: God might decide to judge you with the same yardstick that you used against that other driver. He might even start sending you notes outlining where you are getting it wrong. But he won't put them on your car – he'll put them on your *life*."

Of course we sometimes have to judge – but we need to be sure we do it with God's standards and with God's heart. One of the most powerful illustrations I have ever come across to counter judgmentalism came from a Christian leader whose daughter came home and told him what people in church were saying about a well-known TV evangelist who had fallen in spectacular fashion. She said, "Daddy, everybody's talking about what bad things he has done." Her father put his arm around her and said, "Darling, it's true that he has done bad things. But I want you to know this: if he is truly sorry and asks for forgiveness, God will forgive him."

This father said to me, "I want my daughter to know that it matters when she does wrong – that God is grieved by it. But I also want her to know that, whatever she has done, God will still love her – and there will always be a way back."

I think of another story told to me by a church leader just this week. One of the young people in his church loved playing in the worship band. He was the drummer. The only problem was that this seventeen-year-old's lifestyle outside church was challenging to say the least. He smoked and sometimes drank too much. He was a party animal through and through. His parents were often beside themselves with worry for him, but glad that at least he seemed to love his role in the worship band.

One day a woman approached the church leader and

told him that it was unacceptable for this boy to play in the worship band and that the very fact that he was allowed to do so set a bad example to the other young people in church. I often think that King Solomon was very bright in asking God for wisdom as a gift and every church leader should follow his example, because at times you need all the wisdom that great king had and more. No two situations are the same and there are often no clear right or wrong answers, but the leader on this occasion thought first about this particular young man. What would serve his interests best? What course of action would give him the best possible chance of continuing on and deepening his admittedly very shaky walk with Christ?

He decided that, as the boy was not actually leading the worship, just playing in the band, he would let him continue. Was he right? Who knows? I just thank God that the leader loved this boy enough to wrestle with the issue. Standards are important in church life. But love must always guide how we enforce those standards.

Finally, let's not judge each other by how we think our children are doing. Don't live your life wondering what other Christians are making of your parenting. You may be ashamed of some of the things your children have done, but never be ashamed of *them*.

I remember sitting on a train in the New York subway some years ago. My fellow passengers and I had our heads sunk in our newspapers and looked up only briefly when a young man, who appeared as though he had been sleeping rough, began making a pitch for money. But suddenly he stopped asking us to open our wallets and said, "Ladies and gentlemen, I haven't always been like this. And you should all know that anything can happen to anybody."

As I glanced around the carriage I saw that people had lifted their heads from the sports or fashion pages and were looking intently at him. And I know why. We didn't have just a homeless man trying to raise a little cash in our carriage – we now had a philosopher on the train. And in our hearts we all knew that he was right: *anything can happen to anybody.*

I met recently with Andy, a British church leader, and his wife, who told me of the day they discovered that their sixteen-year-old son, Ben, was taking drugs. Their world was rocked. And it wasn't just because of the drug taking. They had always been close as a family, but all this young man seemed to care about now was staying out half the night with his new set of friends. And it wasn't a flash-in-the-pan experiment: he had become an addict whose memory was affected by his abuse of drugs. Any parent who has experienced the sheer sense of helplessness you can feel when you realize that actually you have no real control at all over your near-adult children will understand something of how these parents felt. Andy said, "What could I do? I suppose I could have told him, 'You'll never live under my roof while you're taking drugs'. But how could I do that to my own son?"

He went on to tell me that he had written a letter to his son. Part of it read, "I hate the way you are living, but I will never stop loving you. I want to grow old with you as one of my best friends. But I am your father and I can't just say to you 'Live as you want.'"

Andy asked Ben to do three things. First, if he was going to stay out all night, that he would at least let them know which of his friends he was going to be with. The boy agreed. Andy then asked him to continue to join them when they prayed as a family and, third, to keep coming to church with them. Ben said, "You can't make me go to church!"

"No," his father replied, "I can't. But I'd like it if you did."

Andy told me he will never forget preaching to an audience of a thousand people and seeing his son in the very back row with his feet draped over the seat in front, leaning back with his eyes closed and listening to music through his ear phones – sometimes spaced out from the night before. He said that he offered to resign as senior pastor three times, but the other leaders urged him to stay.

Not everyone was so understanding. Often people would comment to Ben on the way he was dressed or on the fact that he that wasn't paying attention during the service. Sometimes people would ask one of Andy's other children, "Does your father know what Ben is getting up to?"

But the boy kept coming to church, and when the family prayed together he turned up to be there with them. One day Ben met an older, very conservative Christian whom you would expect to have been the last person to have any influence on him. But God used this man to change his life. Sometimes as parents, when we have done all we can, we need to allow others to step into our children's lives.

Ben is now in his thirties and leads a church in the USA. As I have thought about his journey of rebellion and eventual coming home, I have realized that at heart it came down to a mother and father deciding that, although there was nothing they could do about many of the things in that situation, they would do what they *could.* They could keep on loving, keep on praying, and keep on trying to continue their son's connection with the wider Christian community. And they could ask those they worshipped with to help them do that. On that latter point, some did – and some didn't.

I remember when one of my children did something that saddened me deeply. I said to them, "I'm ashamed of what you've done. But I'm not ashamed of *you.*" We held each other and cried.

A few years ago a Christian leader rang me to tell me that his unmarried daughter was pregnant. He told me how disappointed he was and wondered what he should say to her. I said, "Even if you never say another word about this, she knows what you feel about it. Your task now is to let her know how much you love her and will support her." Some years later he told me that this simple bit of advice had revolutionized his relationship with his daughter. Judgmentalism closes the door... Love knocks.

Chapter 9

Overfamiliarity

"But in Nazareth, where he lived as a child, he could do no mighty work – because of their unbelief."[1]

Cynicism, hypocrisy, judgmentalism – even the words sound hard, but perhaps, even combined, they are not as dangerous as a much softer word. It was this very word that stopped those who had known Jesus more intimately than almost any others from *really* knowing him, *really* loving him. The word is "familiarity".

The good folk of Nazareth had just got too used to Jesus. They saw him every day. When they were young they had played with him in the dusty streets, and later on they had gone to his father's workshop to get the yokes for their oxen made. There was nothing new you could tell them about him.

And so it was that while the people from Capernaum, Bethsaida, Jerusalem, and even the hated Samaritan towns saw the deaf healed, the blind seeing, and even the dead raised, those who had known Jesus almost all his life saw little of that. Whereas others listened to the parables in awe, climbed trees just to get a glimpse of him, or practically broke their backs rowing as fast as they could to be with him on the other side of the lake of Galilee, the people of Nazareth said, "He's just Jesus. He's always been here. Aren't his mother and his sisters still with us?"[2]

There are many blessings in being brought up in a home where the parents know Christ – where his stories are told, where Bibles are strewn about the house, and where the children are taken to the place where people gather together to worship him every Sunday. But an ever-present danger – perhaps even a curse – is that those who enjoy such treasures just get used to them – and to him. It's just Jesus.

Stephen Matthew, the child of Christian parents, is Associate Pastor of Abundant Life Church, Bradford. This is how he put it:

If I can put my battle into one word, it's been with familiarity. It has been with just taking God, church and this good, stable, moral upbringing totally for granted and thinking, "Isn't this a boring way to live!" That has been my major battle. For people like me, the world has a certain attraction. Sin seems really exciting. It looks and sounds as if it's going to be the best fun ever... I had to battle to develop my own strong faith and not just ride on the faith of my parents.[3]

Familiarity robs us of so many things. It robs us of wonder, it robs us of faith, and, perhaps most of all, it robs us of gratitude.

Some time ago Dianne and I were invited for Sunday lunch with some friends. Jack, the husband, has been a Christian for many years; his parents were leaders in a dynamic overseas church and the truth is that he has never strayed far from the fold in which he was nurtured. But in recent years Jack has become cynical and hard. He is quick to criticize preachers and worship leaders, and when someone shares a moment in which they have sensed a touch of God, his face says, "I've heard it all before." But it wasn't until that lunchtime that I saw something else in my friend.

As we were sitting around the table and about to eat he said, "Well, I suppose we'd better say grace." His words seemed to hang in the air. In a world where millions are starving, we were sitting in a warm home at a table laden with food and he said, "We'd better say grace." I may have imagined it, but I almost thought I heard heaven say, "Keep it."

When we get used to Jesus – either as children or as adults – it's not so much that we rebel against him, as that we simply become *used* to him. But I sense that with some young people it is not just overfamiliarity that's the problem, but a sense of inferiority: that because they have lived such a sheltered life they feel their Christian experience is practically worthless.

Listen again to Stephen Matthew:

If you line up a first-generation believer and me on the platform and ask us both to give our testimonies of salvation, who has the better tale? He may tell you about his life of violence, crime, sin and debauchery, and I'm going to tell you what a good, clean-living boy I was! And what's going to inspire people more?

I remember going to hear Nicky Cruz, who features in the book *The Cross and the Switchblade*, speak about how he led a gang in New York. He gave his testimony of killing people, extortion, drug and alcohol excess and so on. We were all gasping in awe. But at the end of it, I felt depressed! Why? Because I thought, "He has been saved from so much more than me. Did I even need saving? Am I worth as much to Jesus as Nicky Cruz?"[4]

I sometimes wonder whether we have been unwise in the way that we have focused so much on the testimonies of celebrities, or whether we have perhaps glamorized the stories of those who had particularly wild lives in the past. This has led some young people to feel that what they have to share about themselves is not worth listening to: that the story of somebody who isn't famous or wasn't an out-and-out rebel is not worth telling.

Can we, as parents, encourage our kids to see that their testimony is exciting? If God has been a part of their experience since they were very young, then that is something to rejoice over. Instead of expecting testimonies to be about sin, let's start telling stories of how God has been able to use people – all kinds of people. Instead of talking about what we have done wrong, let's talk about what God has done *right*.

How can we prevent our children from becoming so familiar with Jesus that they forget to take their shoes off on holy ground? I wish I knew. But it must have at least something to do with us – their parents – somehow keeping that sense of awe.

I remember somebody telling me that the way to discover how much you love something is to imagine it gone for ever. Once in a while I try to imagine Jesus gone for ever from my life: no forgiveness; no hope; no one to listen to the desperate prayers that even I find easy to pray when I am at my wits' end; no heaven to come; no light in the darkness; no one to pick me up when I fall, dust me down and send me on again. And when I think of that I have an ache in my very soul and a great anguish for my children lest I have ever made it easy for them to take him for granted.

By God's grace, may we as parents help our children to maintain a healthy awe of God. An awe that will keep them from becoming so familiar with him that they forget who he is and say, in essence, "Oh, he's been around our home for ever...

...that's just Jesus."

I remember being a young Christian. Life was relatively simple: God loved you and you loved God. You went to hear Christian bands, read books about drug dealers becoming believers, went to the Christian Union in school, and thought you knew most of the answers to the big questions of life and death. Although you tried your best to be humble, you were pretty sure that, if God had an A-team, you were on it.

And then the years went by. Your best friend got cancer and you prayed for her to be well and believed God had healed her; but you remember the cold rainy day when you stood and cried at the graveside. One of the drug dealers who had been miraculously converted went back to dealing. Some of the sure-fire answers you had to the big questions began to wobble a little. And, worst of all, you realized that reading the Bible and living it were quite different things; you weren't quite the spiritual giant you had thought you were.

And so into a young life crept the great killer of faith: disappointment. Perhaps it had to come, but did it need to arrive with such devastating power? Wasn't it possible for someone to have helped get us ready for the day when it tried to destroy our fragile faith – to have warned us? Did it need to come upon us as such a surprise? Couldn't a parent, a youth worker, a church leader have got us ready for the three disappointments that will, at some time, stalk into the lives of every follower of Jesus. The next three chapters deal with each in turn: Disappointment with Others; Disappointment with Ourselves; and Disappointment with God.

Chapter 10

Get Them Ready for Disappointment with Others

When we are young, we believe. We listen to preachers and we believe. We sing along with worship leaders and we believe. We rub shoulders with strong Christians from our church and we believe. And why would we not believe? The preachers are famous (at least in *our* world), the worship leaders seem to practically visit heaven when they sing, and the strong Christians from our church have been, well – strong – as long as we have known them.

In fact, when we are young our belief goes even deeper than that. Our heroes of the faith, both local and worldwide, come to epitomize God. It's not surprising. These men and women tell us what God thinks, what hurts him, what pleases him, and the way to live a life that will honour him. We aspire to be like them. In some ways they are almost Jesus to us.

But they are *not* Jesus. And if we are to help our children get through to a mature faith, we are going to have to get them ready for a devastating day. It's the day when they will have to hold on to faith in God despite being disappointed with others. They are going to have to still trust God when his followers let them down.

I spoke recently with a father, Paul. He told me of the time it was discovered that one of the leaders from his church was having an affair. The leader had been among those who started the church and it had grown from a congregation of just a handful of people to over four hundred. He had preached, led Bible studies, engaged in evangelism and appeared on television on behalf of that church. But, more than that, this leader had been like a second father to Paul's children. He had played with them when they were small and he had prayed with them when they were teenagers. In the otherwise uncertain world of a child, this man was a rock of faith.

Paul told me of the evening that he had broken the news of the leader's affair to his fourteen-year-old daughter. He said, "We went for a walk together and I told her what had happened as gently as I could. But nothing prepared me for the strength of her reaction. At first, she cried and said, 'But, Daddy, he's a *Christian.*' And then she went silent. She just didn't want to talk about it any more – not later that night or in her older teenage years. It was almost as if her faith died that night."

A friend of mine who is a youth leader took several of the teenagers from his church to a large youth event at which they were shown a film that was truly amazing. The subject of the film was a Christian leader who was seriously ill with cancer and yet here he was, singing a worship song he'd written himself. He sang with life-saving plastic tubes in his nose and the lyrics came out from behind an oxygen mask. The song was called "Healer".

The kids were blown away. Here was a living example of praising God in all circumstances. How could they ever complain again of the minor persecutions they had to face at school because they were followers of Jesus? Here, at last, was a picture they could never forget of vibrant faith that believed for wholeness even while whispering the words through an oxygen mask.

But this Christian leader didn't have cancer, and whatever the reasons were for what he did, the whole episode was a sham. When the true story broke the youth leader tried to pick up the pieces with the kids who had watched that film. But it wasn't easy; they were devastated. One child said, "I will never trust anyone again. I will never take anyone at face value."

Another friend has fallen out with a rather vociferous part of the Christian community that disagrees with his theology. They have let him and others know of their disapproval in no uncertain terms. It is true that they have spoken plainly, and they are to be commended for that, but in much of it there has been an apparent lack of any grace or genuine love for him.

When I spoke to my friend about the letters, the phone calls and, especially, some of the emails he had received, he said a fascinating thing: "My greatest worry is not for me or even for my wife. It is for my children. They are watching parts of the Christian community tear their father apart. The sheer vitriol is staggering. I worry for them and what they will think of Jesus."

I can understand how that father felt the night he told his teenage daughter about their friend's affair. I can sympathize with the church youth leader as he tried to pick up the pieces after a Christian "celebrity" went off the rails. And my heart goes out to the friend who has managed to get on the wrong end of some biting criticism given "in love" and his worry for his children.

Those are hard situations to face.

But if you asked me where I have seen the greatest and deepest disillusionment of young people with other Christians I would have to say it is in ordinary, everyday church life. As we stamp and kick in church AGMs or news gets out of the slanging match at the PCC, when we gossip about each other or make biting comments because somebody has offended us in some small way, we think we are getting away with it. But the scary thing about children isn't that they don't listen to us, but that they *do*. Every word counts. Every action is formative. *Nothing* is lost.

Just this week a man I had not met for some time said to me, "Our church has just been through a split." We say this as though it's nothing – as if such things are just part of belonging to the Christian community. I have never visited that church. I have no direct knowledge of what caused the fracture that sent half of them one way and the other half the other. And yet I can "smell" that split. I can almost hear the early rumblings over the issues of the new building programme, the style of worship, the way that the leaders are chosen, or the youth work. You don't have to show me the letters that were furtively pushed through leaders' doors or offer to let me read the emails that scattered their venom across the atmosphere.

We have become used to the phrase "collateral damage". It is a euphemism for "non-combatant casualties" – itself a euphemism for civilians being shredded by exploding bombs. When churches fight and split there is always "collateral damage". It should not be a surprise to us; Jesus could not have been clearer: when we live lives that do not demonstrate love towards each other, it is very difficult for people to see us as genuine followers of Jesus. That lack of love affects not only our faith, but theirs. Jesus said, "By this everyone will know you are my disciples, if you love one another."[1]

And when one half of the church tries to start again in the half-empty building and the others begin a new church a few miles away, the split may soon be forgotten. But not by all. So often it is the children that are the collateral damage. Like kids who stand open-mouthed as their parents divorce, so these children watch aghast as their spiritual home is torn apart.

As I have presented "Bringing Home the Prodigals" events around the world, parents from many and varied cultures have told me of their pain over children who have walked away from God. But the most moving conversations have often been not with parents but with the "prodigals" themselves, as they shared from their heart what drove them away from the faith.

I found that often their stories were not of sex, drugs or rock 'n' roll. It wasn't the lure of the "far country" that had inched them away from the father's house; it was more prosaic than that. So-called prodigal after prodigal told me that they had simply become disillusioned with Christians – with the "infighting" and the way Christians treated each other – and they had decided that, if that was how church life was, they couldn't go on following Christ.

But, let's face it, it's not just other people with whom our children may become disillusioned: it is with us, their parents. When our kids are very young we may seem like God to them. But the day will come, sooner or later, when it will dawn on them that we are not. And, bit by bit, the image they have of the father or mother who can do no wrong will be demolished. This could happen over many years or in one fell swoop – but it will surely happen. In many ways it is good that it does, but, depending on how we have taught our children, the results can be quite different.

On the one hand, there can easily be total devastation that the parents they thought were perfect – and who themselves strove to portray a picture of perfection – have let them down. But if we are wise we will always have spoken of our vulnerability, acknowledged our weakness, and spent years trying to get our children to focus not on us but on Jesus.

In the light of this, what can we do as parents to help stop our children from being sandbagged by the crushing blow of disappointment with others? The first thing is to be real. Don't assume that your child will get through life untouched by any of this stuff. Don't believe that the "Christian celebrities" they come across will all be good influences. Don't imagine that somebody they respect in your Christian community could not turn their back on faith in some spectacular way. Don't think for a moment that some people in your church will not treat your child badly, or that your child won't ever have to watch those who are part of the body of Christ tearing each other apart. And tell them before it happens that, one day, we – their parents – may well disappoint both them and God.

Tell them also that, although all this grieves God, it is not a shock to him. Tell them that the Bible is littered with the stories of God-followers who got it wrong: from Abraham to Moses, from Gideon to David, from James to John, from Peter to Paul. Tell them that other Christians will let them down, as they themselves might well let others down. But help them to see that this does not mean that *God* is letting them down. And help them also to understand that because God forgives us time and time again, we too need sometimes to be a little easier on others.

Do all you can to ensure that your children's faith and their foundation is in Jesus himself. Tell them that others may betray them, but he will not. Tell them that Christians can be fickle, but with him "there is not even the shadow that turning causes".[2] Tell them to keep their eyes on Jesus – the one who began it all and the one who will end it all.

Tell them this not so they forget for a moment the challenge of becoming more like Jesus – we are meant to be expressions of his life: salt and light, grace and truth, holiness and compassion. But tell them so that on the day that is surely coming when the tempter says to them, "Look what they have done to you. Why would you follow a God like that?", they will be able to say, "It is true they have hurt me. But I have learned this lesson...

...they are not Jesus."

Chapter 11

Get Them Ready for Disappointment with Themselves

What is the great longing of our heart? I have no doubt it is the endeavour to prove we are worth loving. For many of us, this compulsion is all-consuming. Life screams at us: "You must be clever to be loved"; "You must be beautiful to be loved"; "You must be sexy to be loved"; "You must be wealthy to be loved".

But life can have no idea how cruel it is to scream such things. Does it not know that already our heart doubts that we are worthy of love? Can it not tell that, let alone the need for more brilliance, attractiveness, and money, we are already scrabbling together our meagre store of offerings and whispering in our souls, "No, I'm not worth loving." Our worthlessness wraps itself around us like a chain. It seems we cannot be free of it: we are imprisoned.

And then we come to Christ and discover the truth of unconditional love. But, although for a while the freedom is wonderful, the old insecurities come flooding back. Soon we find ourselves struggling, and again we feel the need to prove ourselves. But this time it's not to other people but to God himself that we feel the need to prove we are worth loving. We strive to show our devotion, our piety, or our commitment to his service. But there is little peace here, for it is a wearisome business being good or busy enough to earn God's love.

When Lynne Hybels, wife of Bill Hybels, the pastor of Willow Creek Church, one day rediscovered the true God instead of the tyrant image she had grown up with, she felt him say to her, "I wasn't the one cracking the whip, the one telling you to work harder, the one who made you feel guilty when you relaxed. I was the one who saw you, who knew you, who believed in you... I was the one trying to love you."[1]

She was free at last.

Many Christians never experience this freedom. The enemy of our souls is called the Accuser, and we can be haunted all our life by the dreadful condemnation that we are nothing more than an ongoing disappointment to God. So often this insecurity combines with the propensity of human beings to devise rules and regulations by which we may judge others and ourselves, and we are soon carrying out a daily checklist of whether we are or are not good followers of Jesus.

I believe that many people who have been Christians for a long time have learned to live with this. If they have a daily quiet time they feel close to God, but if they miss it they feel condemned. If they see outward success in the work they do for God they feel his blessing, but if it goes badly they feel it is probably their fault and that God is trying to teach them something. This is not a new problem; two thousand years ago Paul wrote: "Are you so foolish? After beginning with the Spirit, are you now trying to attain your goal by human effort?"[2]

For many young people, this experience is enough to kill their faith. They simply cannot live with the sense of failure they feel in the task of following Jesus. They sit in church and see others actively engaged in worship but they don't feel the same enthusiasm. They try hard to read the Bible but find it boring. They find it difficult to share their faith with their friends – in fact they sometimes feel embarrassed about admitting they go to church.

I think of a boy of fourteen who came under

incredible pressure from his parents to "share his faith" with his schoolmates. They told him that the Bible says that if he was ashamed of Jesus, then Jesus would be ashamed of him. He tried – boy, how he tried! – but it always turned out disastrously.

His father also told him that the Bible says the Holy Spirit would give him the words he needed. If that was true, he must have swallowed them, because he always spluttered his way through his every evangelistic effort. And, one day, as he was leaving school having tried to talk to a very pretty girl who had asked him if he thought she was going to hell, he said under his breath, "I'm not going to do this any more." He knew that he had let God down: Jesus was ashamed of him.

Nobody in his home or church was honest with him. Nobody told him that actually many adults in the congregation who had been followers of Jesus for years struggled to share their faith easily with others, and that, although we all have to be ready to tell people what we believe, there are some who seem to have a special gift for it.

Because nobody told him the truth – just quoted out-of-context verses at him that seemed to suggest it was all a walk in the park – he assumed that there was something wrong with him as a Christian. Because he was young, he had no way of challenging that. And so he gave up following Christ altogether – not because he didn't love God, but rather, as he put it to his youth leader, because "I'm a crap Christian."

Of course what these kids don't know is that many people who have been Christians for years feel exactly as they do. The difference is, they have learned to hide it from others and, as far as their own hearts are concerned, to live with it. Young people are often much more black and white in their thinking. They reason, "If I find all this so hard, it must be because I'm not really a Christian – or at least not a very good one." And so they give up.

Sometimes I think we simply forget how fragile the faith of the young can be. One young woman I spoke to said, "I stopped going to church because I had doubts about my faith and I thought that I couldn't possibly be a good Christian and not be absolutely sure about it all." When I listened to her I could have cried – at the honesty, at the torment she must have gone through, and at the incredible tragedy that nobody had told her how very normal – perhaps even necessary – it is to doubt.

In some ways, many of those we consider to be "prodigals" simply have a keener sense of failure, and sometimes sin, than others who appear never to go off the straight and narrow. Sometimes as parents we compound this sense of failure, particularly so when we judge our children by the unofficial list of "Top Ten Sins" that many churches hold. In this list, sexual wrong is seen as the very worst.

I remember speaking with a father who told me that his daughter simply could not forgive herself for the fact that she had slept with a boyfriend some years previously. He said, "Of course, my wife and I were devastated by her doing that, and we talked about it a lot, but we are learning to live with it."

I said, "I can't help thinking that perhaps your ongoing attitude to what happened is affecting your daughter. The key to her being able to forgive herself is for you and your wife to put this in the past. When your daughter truly believes that you have let it go, she will more easily be able to accept God's forgiveness and move on herself."

One of the greatest mistakes we make in dealing with our children's failures is when we become over-concerned about what the Christian community will make of them. Our son gets drunk one night after a party at a friend's house and is seen rolling home by some of the members of our church who enjoy – a little too much – telling us what they have seen. We are mortified. We say to ourselves, "What will people think of us?" And because of that we totally over-react to what has happened. We make our son feel as if, in God's eyes, he has committed the equivalent of mass murder. But he hasn't. It is true he has made a mistake, and it is also true that we're going to have to deal with it, but it's important to put the event in a realistic context.

So what can we do to help young people facing experiences like this? The answer is not easy. We don't help them by simply throwing in the towel and saying, "Anything goes. Live as you want. Do what you want. God will still love you." Max Lucado puts it well: "God loves you just the way you are, but he refuses to leave you that way. He wants you to be just like Jesus."[3]

But at the same time we must teach our young people that all heroes and heroines of the Bible, with the exception of Jesus, are men and women who, while striving to please God, often got it wrong – sometimes spectacularly. And yet somehow they found the forgiveness, grace and strength to dust themselves off and stand up again. We must tell the stories of the failures – of Peter's denial, of Paul and Barnabas' arguments, of David's infidelity, of James and John's pride. In other words, while motivating them to be the best they can be for Christ, we have to get them ready for disappointment with themselves.

One of the ways we can help in this as parents is to let

our children see how we deal with situations in which we feel we could have done better. It could be in little things – letting them see when we're annoyed with ourselves over the way we yelled at the other driver who cut us up, or it could be in matters of huge importance – such as the way we handled the breakdown of our marriage. I have often told my children of occasions when I felt I let God down and how it made me feel. I told them of those times even when they were young enough to think their father was probably perfect.

Did I want to be a good example to them? Yes. Did I want my life to be an encouragement for them to press on with following Jesus? Yes. Did I want to present to them a picture of somebody who seemed to have it all together? No. A thousand times no. I wanted them to see how I dealt with failure. I wanted them to see how I ran to God and in spirit knelt before the cross and asked for forgiveness. And I wanted them to learn that, although we may feel that we are often a disappointment to God, we are never a surprise to him.

I wanted them to be able to come up against times in life when they felt they were wretched failures – and not give up. I wanted them to grasp the incredible power of the cross of Christ to bring forgiveness and healing of the soul. I wanted them to realize that, "If our hearts condemn us, God is greater than our hearts."[4]

I wanted them to be able to be disappointed with themselves and be convicted of their wrong. I wanted them to be disappointed with themselves and have a desire to change. I wanted them to be disappointed with themselves and for that to lead to a longing for holiness. But, as well as that, I wanted them to be able to go through times in life when they were disappointed with themselves...

...and still survive.

Chapter 12

Get Them Ready for Disappointment with God

Lily is five years old and her goldfish, aptly (if not originally) named Goldie, is ill. At least Goldie *looks* ill. Lily wants you to scan the internet for remedies, but you're a parent – you've seen at least six fish come and go and in your heart you know that this one is not going to pull through: by tomorrow there'll be another matchbox buried in the garden.

But that evening, as you say prayers with Lily, she comes up with a better plan. "Mummy, why don't we just ask Jesus to make Goldie better?" And before you can mention the inevitability of death which touches every creature, little eyes are screwed tightly shut and young lips are fervently praying, "Dear Jesus, please,

please, please make Goldie better. Thank you. Amen." Lily opens her eyes and smiles at you. "I know he'll do it, Mummy. Night night."

You close her bedroom door and leap down the stairs two at a time. As you hit the hallway you are yelling into the living room, "What time does Pet World close?" But you don't wait for an answer. You are a mother on a mission, and if necessary you'll break into the place. You actually hear the rear wheels of your car skid as you roar away, but then you suddenly panic and throw the car into reverse. You rush back into the house, grab your mobile phone and take a photograph.

When you get there, you realize that you needn't have worried about the store being closed. The cavernous building that sells everything from hamster beds to poop scoopers for Great Danes is not only open, but positively humming with activity. In fact it takes a while to find a sales assistant who's free, but when you do, you know you've hit gold. This young man positively oozes both love for animals and deep care for hassled mothers. "How can I help you?" he says. You pull out your mobile and show him the screen: "I need a goldfish that looks *exactly* like this one."

If you thought he would laugh, you were wrong. He's been a part of this little scene a dozen times. "Well, madam," he says, leading the way to the aquarium, "let's see what we can do…"

The following morning Lily is up even earlier than usual, and when she runs into the kitchen you are just getting breakfast ready. She doesn't even say hello – just rushes straight to the goldfish bowl and peers in. And then she yells, "Mummy, he's done it! He's made Goldie well. And he's even made him fatter!"

You meant well and, who knows, perhaps on this occasion you even *did* well. But for every parent who wants their child to develop a faith that will survive the long haul, there is an even greater responsibility than making life right for him or her. We have to prepare them for a truly terrifying moment. It is terrifying because, until that moment comes, God has "never let them down" – he has made Daddy's cough better and provided a sunny day for the birthday party; he has blessed thousands of people all across the world and always answered our prayers to guard us while we sleep. *We have to get them ready for the day when they are disappointed with God.*

Listen in to Bart Simpson's prayer life. It's Christmas Eve. "O God, if you bring me lots of good stuff tomorrow, I promise not to do anything bad between now and when I wake up." Bart's "deal" with God may make us smile, but perhaps this is not just an issue for kids. Could it be that unwittingly we are living our lives with the unspoken belief that we have a secret "deal" with God?

It goes something like this: "God, I will follow you, serve and love you, but in return you will look after me. A little pain, some persecution that doesn't get too nasty, and minor family traumas are all accepted as part of my sanctification. But that's it. No failing marriages, children who turn their backs on church, illnesses that kill those I love, or redundancies that don't ultimately lead to a more fulfilling job."

I remember meeting a man in his mid-forties some years ago. He had been a Christian for years and had seemed to live a charmed life. He had a lovely home and a wonderful family, was financially secure, and had been given talent in abundance. Tom was good at everything. And then one day he was made redundant. But his job wasn't the only thing Tom lost that day: he lost his faith in God. He has never been inside a church since. He said to a friend, "If there was a God who loved me, he wouldn't have let this happen to me."

Don't be too hard on him. You and I may not know how we will react when we experience what Dr R. T. Kendall calls "the seeming betrayal of God". The theme of the "deal" is, of course, at the heart of the drama in the oldest book in the Bible: how will Job's love for God hold up when it seems that God is not keeping his end of the bargain?

When life is good we will believe – even praise – God. But when trouble comes we may struggle dreadfully. I think now of a Christian leader who has been blessed in so many areas, but harder times have now come and his wife says, "He is not the man he used to be."

My mind goes to a group of people praying for a friend to be healed; she is dying before their eyes. Do they have enough faith? I tell you, I believe with all my heart that they do. But now they are beginning to say, "What are we doing wrong?" "What are we not claiming?" "Which of us does not have enough faith?"

I think of a woman whose son has broken her heart. At times it seems that the wound is so great it will take her life. She mourns. She is a wonderful mother; she is a woman of great faith, and nobody has prayed more for their child.

How will these people cope with being disappointed by God?

Some years ago I was speaking at a weekend conference hosted by Care for the Family, the UK charity I work with. It was a retreat for parents who had children with especially challenging needs. Some of these children had eating disorders, some were addicted to illegal drugs, and some had severe physical or emotional challenges. I had been speaking elsewhere on Friday evening and by the time I arrived at the conference on Saturday morning the event was in full swing. As I approached the room where they were meeting I heard a worship song being sung. I went in, slipped into the back row and joined in with those who were singing.

I had only been there for a minute or two when the woman in front of me began to cry uncontrollably and then rushed out of the room. I followed her. When we were outside I said, "What's wrong? How can I help you?" It took her a while to talk but then she told me her story. Her name was Jan. Her son had been a drug addict and one day, in a dispute over money, his dealers had set him alight. They had eventually been arrested and then he had been due to give evidence against them in court. She had begged him not to, but he had said he was staying with a friend and that his attackers would never find him.

Jan told me that, on the morning of the case, the police had turned up at her house to say her son had not arrived in court. She went searching for him and found him dead in a squat. A man who lived there had discovered his body and told her that shortly before that he had seen two men running away from the house. Jan said the police were trying to establish whether her son had overdosed accidentally, taken his own life, or been murdered. I tried to comfort her and prayed with her, and we both went back into the main room.

As I was going to be speaking shortly after this, I took a seat in the front row. A young woman in her late twenties was speaking. This is what she said:

My husband, Neil, and I desperately wanted children and were thrilled beyond words when I became pregnant. When our baby was born, we found she had Down's syndrome and then, when she was two years old, my husband died. My daughter is now six.

The other day I was sitting in our garden, praying with a friend from church who is ill. Suddenly my little girl came out of the house and ran up to us. She smiled at my friend and put her hand on my friend's arm. And then she put her other hand in the air and began praying for my friend to be made well.

As I sat and listened I looked down at the notes for the talk I had planned to give. It didn't look as good as when I had prepared it the week before. I remember thinking, "What on earth can I say to these people?"

I never did preach the message I had prepared. Instead I said, "Some of you have disabled children, don't you? And some have children with other challenging needs?" They nodded. "And you wish they were completely well, don't you?" They nodded again. "But you love them *anyway*, don't you?" A third nod of their heads. I think they thought I was about to say, "That's how God loves you. He loves you *anyway*." But I said, "That's *how you love God*. You don't love God simply because all your prayers are answered and all your dreams are fulfilled. You love him *anyway*."

I went on, "I hear Christians say, 'God has been so good to me. He has blessed my family, my business, my career, my church. I love him so much.' But circumstances like these are not the test of love. The test is when we can say, along with an old prophet, 'Though the fig-tree does not bud and there are no grapes on the vines, though the olive crop fails and the fields produce no food… yet I will rejoice in the Lord.'[1] I know that sometimes to love God like that is hard, and that you must have many doubts and fears, and that you sometimes worry that your love is not strong enough. But do you see how precious love like that is to him?"

Someone started to cry… I started to cry… soon we were all crying.

One of the most powerful phrases in the whole Bible is tucked away at the heart of the book of Daniel. Three young men are threatened by King Nebuchadnezzar that if they do not bow down to an idol they will be thrown into a furnace. They refuse to obey and say, "If we are thrown into the blazing furnace, the God we serve is able to save us from it… *But even if he does not,* we want you to know, O king, that we will not serve your gods…"[2] Their faith in God was not based on always getting what they wanted; they had learned to trust – "if not".

Part of the task of parents – and churches – is to prepare young people for the day when they will be disappointed with God. Yet so often we fail to do this. We emphasize occasions when our prayers have been answered and gloss over times when it appears that heaven has said no. Sometimes we perform theological gymnastics in an effort to explain away the fact that God seems to have let us down – we appear to see it as our responsibility to make God look good.

I remember when my dear friend, the author Rob Lacey, was dying. Somebody said to him, "Well, at least God allowed you to be well enough to finish your latest book." Rob replied, "Try telling that to my wife and kids." God doesn't need us to defend him.

"God is awesome!" said the preacher. "He can do

anything!" That's true of course, but, even so, sometimes in life we don't get what we want. Not all our cancers are healed; not all our businesses are saved from financial ruin; not all our children turn out as we want; not every examination is passed. At some point in our Christian life we will have to work through a situation in which it seems that God didn't answer our prayers – or at least not in the way we wanted. This was true even for Jesus. In the Garden of Gethsemane he prayed, "Father… take this cup from me."[3] He didn't want to go to the cross. But just a few hours later he said to his disciples, "The cup that the Father has given me – I must drink it."[4] God had said no to his son.

Tell the stories of faith to your children at home and in church. Walk them through the great hall of faith in the eleventh chapter of the book of Hebrews. Talk of the triumphs of Abel, Enoch, Noah, Abraham, Gideon, Samson, David and Samuel: "They shut the mouths of lions, quenched the flames of fire… they escaped death by the edge of the sword… women received their loved ones back again from death."[5]

It is vital that we tell our children those stories, old and new; it will help them to grasp the greatness of their God. But don't stop there in the hall of faith – give them an even deeper foundation. Read on in Hebrews 11:

"But others trusted God and were tortured, some were mocked, others were chained in dungeons… hungry, oppressed and mistreated."[6] Tell them the stories of the "if nots".

There is another reason why we must be prepared for disappointment with God, and it is linked to disappointment with ourselves. So often, when we do not get answers to our prayers, our dreams are not fulfilled, or life suddenly goes badly wrong, we not only say in our hearts, "God has let me down", but we also whisper "I have let God down. If I were a better Christian he would not allow me to go through these circumstances. He may even be punishing me." But we need to understand that in this life bad things happen to good people – people like Abraham and Job, people like John and Peter, and even somebody like Jesus.

Unless we grasp this truth we are vulnerable to the age-old taunt of the enemy of our souls: "If he loved you, this would not be happening."

When my kids were small they had a Bible story book that contained a pop-up version of the story of Daniel in the lions' den. We read it often. It was a chance to tell them of God's ability to rescue those he loves from danger. But as they grew older I found the need to remind both them and myself of those parts in the Bible that it's hard to cover in pop-up versions. When examinations were failed, young hearts broken and dreams sometimes didn't come true, I wanted my kids not to feel so disappointed with God that they lost their love for him. I wanted them to hold on to the certainty of his love. If my illness is healed, I am loved – and if it is *not* healed, I am loved. If I pass the examinations, I am loved – and if I fail them all, I am loved. I am loved: nothing in earth or heaven can change that.

I wanted my children never to lose the understanding that we can cry out to God in any circumstance of life and ask for what we want. But I also wanted them to know that, if we really love him, then sometimes we also have to whisper:

"But if not..."

Our time together is almost over – just two more chapters and a final word! We say "last but not least" and in this case it's true, for the subjects we consider as we close are fundamental to our task.

There is an incredible poster of Taylor Knox, a surfer, in front of a huge wave (over fifty feet high!) at Todos Santos in Mexico. Underneath are the words: "What if your fears and dreams existed in the same place? ... Would you still go there?"

Our penultimate chapter deals largely with our fear and whether it causes us to protect our children to the point where we actually make life more dangerous for them in the long run.

*And the last chapter? Our children's dreams – and whether we can help give them one big enough to **really get their attention**.*

Chapter 13

Get Them Ready for the Real World

In their book *Family Fears*,[1] Jack and Jerry Schreur talk of the five fears that stalk the minds of so many parents:

- The fear that our children will make a life-dominating mistake;
- The fear that our children will not turn out "right";
- The fear that we are failing as a family;
- The fear that we will lose our children through illness or serious accident;
- The fear that our children will not live according to our values and beliefs.

Fear is not always a bad thing, but when it takes us over – when it causes our minds to run away with visions of catastrophe in our children's lives – then so often the result is the same: we overprotect them. We reason thus: "The world is a dangerous and hostile place and there are many traps that my child can fall into – therefore I will protect him or her in all possible ways."

In some nations the Christian subculture is so highly developed that it is possible to cosset one's children in what some have called a "Christian ghetto". We can send our children to a Christian school, they have Christian friends, they attend a Christian youth group, and they read Christian books. They watch Christian television and films and listen to Christian music. They go on holidays to Christian camps and when they leave school they attend a Christian university. And even in countries where all this is not possible, we can still so organize their lives (if they are the kind who will let us!) that in many ways we feel they are "protected" from a hostile world.

Let's not criticize all this too harshly. The truth is that many of these Christian things can be an enormous blessing to our children. In that sense it is not the individual entities that are at issue. No, the problem comes when we, as parents or as churches, are driven not by the opportunity of the blessing that these things can bring, but by an unreasonable fear of the alternatives. And because we are driven by this fear we try to arrange our children's lives so that they are *totally* protected. Having said that, it's easy to sympathize with parents who are bombarded by warnings of how bad the world is. But does God want us to live in that kind of fear?

Is the world a dangerous place? Yes. Are there many and varied temptations for young people? Without a doubt. Is there a culture of easy sex, alcohol and drugs? Absolutely. Is the world worse than it has ever been? Probably not.

Fear should not be our driving force. Some parts of the Christian community seem to thrive on doomsday predictions – as though even God were worried. Do you remember the tremendous fear that gripped the world on the eve of the new millennium? The questions then were about what effect it would have on our computers and why software programmers had not allowed for the numerical certainty of the magic figure 2000? The concern was so great that the issue became known as "Y2K". An article in one magazine was entitled "Y2K chaos and why should you care".

It suggested three scenarios:

- Brown Out: temporary interruptions in many services for up to several months – something like the aftermath of a major hurricane;

- Black Out: prolonged interruptions in many services for a period of years – something like the great depression on a global scale;

- Wipe Out: the collapse of civilization and the end of the world as we know it – picture a total breakdown and restructuring of society.

Newsweek magazine referred to it as "the day the world shuts down".[2] The one bright spot was that on New Year's Eve 1999 the price of air tickets fell. If all the computers were going to fail, not many people wanted to be at thirty thousand feet when it happened. Some churches and ministries seemed to be in the forefront of those predicting chaos. One American church in the late 1990s started what they called the "Joseph Project" to stockpile food so they wouldn't starve when disaster came. Apparently they are still trying to work out what to do with all those beans.

I read of one computer professional who was overseeing the Y2K project at a hospital. In all the testing his company had done they were finding very few problems. As he discussed it with other companies the same picture was emerging. He contacted the leaders at his church and one Sunday evening they tried to try to put things in perspective from both a technological and a theological perspective. They read the following passage together:

> Therefore I tell you, do not worry about your life, what you will eat or drink; or about your body, what you will wear. Is not life more important than food, and the body more important than clothes? Look at the birds of the air; they do not sow or reap or store away in barns, and yet your heavenly Father feeds them. Are you not much more valuable than they? Who of you by worrying can add a single hour to his life?[3]

The IT specialist told those in church that night that he had been in touch with major companies including banks, the local gas, electricity, water and phone companies, and representatives from Wal-Mart. The indications from all of them were that there would be no problems from a millennium bug. And, anyway, if Wal-Mart was open, what more could anyone need? But despite these assurances many in the congregation would not be persuaded. And as he went on to share this message with other Christian groups, he found that many were downright cross.

Why on earth was this? Maybe we have learned to

"love" fear. But, if we do, we will view the world not as somewhere we can be salt and light, but as an alien place with which we should have as little interaction as possible and from which we should escape at the earliest opportunity.

Having this view of life makes us try to protect our children totally from the world and "hunker down" for the whole of their young lives. But, in doing so, we will do them a great disservice in at least two areas. First, when the day comes, as it surely will, when they have to step outside the cocoon, the shock for some will be so severe that they will never recover. And, second, they will have such a distorted view of the world that they will not be able to recognize real danger when they see it.

This is how one youth leader put it:

If your fifteen-year-old is leading the worship band, never misses the church youth club and spends her time totally within the confines of church and the Christian Union at school, you may want to rejoice. But you should also realize the enormity of the shock that may hit her when she enters the wider world – perhaps when she goes to university.

When people in my church heard that I was going to university to study theology, they were concerned.

Conversations went something like this: "Don't you think that's going to make you lose your faith? I know a guy who went to study theology and he's an atheist now…"

And after I'd got my theology degree, people tended to ask me whether studying theology had made me "question" my faith, or whether I'd been under pressure to stop believing. The impression I got was that people saw theology as the discipline of destroying faith.

But no one ever asks whether a young churchgoing adult should go off and study chemistry, or engineering, or law, or English Literature. And yet plenty of believing young people leave home to study those subjects and somewhere along the way they lose their faith. From my experience – based on the number of people in the Christian Union who were studying it – the only "safe subject" is Town Planning!

While it's true that some people do "lose their faith" as a result of studying theology, far more lose their faith as a result of "studying" full stop. The university lifestyle with its emphasis on "freedom" – drinking, clubbing, "safe sex", and occasional coursework – is more seductive than a dry lecture on Logical Positivism. I meet few people who claim to have lost their faith because of reading Bultmann's theory of demythologizing Scripture. But I meet plenty of people who stopped going to church because they were hung-over on Sunday mornings.

And university isn't the hardest place for a young adult to be a Christian. Unlike the average workplace, universities have chaplaincies and Christian Unions, and often several churches operating student ministries. It is their first job – whether it's a Saturday shift in a supermarket or a graduate training scheme – that will bring them into contact with a huge range of people from all kinds of background and with little or no support from Christians.

One young woman put it like this:

I spent a stint working a second job in a cinema, alongside several sixteen- to eighteen-year-olds. Whilst they were all great people, I saw first-hand how difficult it is to be the one Christian in that age bracket. The friends I made were obsessed with fashion, sex and drinking. Many took pride in avoiding hard work. Some were blatantly and

shamelessly stealing from the company, making a joke
of the fact they were pinching stuff. The main social
activity was to go clubbing when the shifts finished
after midnight, with the added assumption that, if
you went clubbing, you went to "pull".

We are not meant to be terrified of the world. The ten
"spies" in Canaan were not really spies. The word in the
original means to "explore" – they were not sent out to
spy out a threat, but to catalogue an opportunity. It's
just that ten of them turned into spies and they reported
what they saw so as to incite panic and fear. Bad news
travels fast, and misery loves company. It reminds me of
the word of God to the Israelites:

> As for those of you who are left, I will make their
> hearts so fearful in the lands of their enemies that the
> sound of a wind-blown leaf will put them to flight.
> They will run as though fleeing from the sword, and
> they will fall, even though no-one is pursuing them.[4]

Before they had the cartographical instruments they
have now, map-makers would painstakingly draw maps
of the places they had explored. At the edges of the map
they would write, "Beyond this there may be dragons."

They had never seen a dragon, and there had never been a dragon in any of the territories they had managed to penetrate, but beyond the edge of the map was the future and the future was unknown. When the explorers actually went to these new places they were often areas of wonderful beauty, rich in resources and opportunity, but, until they did, they were represented by those six words at the edge of a map: "Beyond this there may be dragons."

We have to learn to let go of the fear and to face the responsibility of helping our children get ready to deal with life in the real world. Let me mention some ways we can do this.

We can get them ready for the day when they won't have us around to help them make decisions. Part of that task is to help them discern for themselves between right and wrong. Instead of trying to convince our children that the only music worth listening to is the Christian sort, help them to develop the critical faculties that will enable them to make wise decisions about what they listen to. One young person said:

There was a huge emphasis in my youth group one summer on listening to rock music. We all had to watch a video called "Hell's Bells", which warned of the dangers of rock music and included clips of several AC/DC songs. I know that at least three members of the group went out and bought AC/DC albums as a result because they enjoyed the clips on the video. If our youth leaders had just said, "AC/DC? They're for boring old people!" then most of us wouldn't have bothered with them at all.

We should allow our children to have friends outside the Christian community – perhaps people they meet at their Saturday job in the pizza parlour, not just those they see when they help out in the Christian bookshop. Don't assume that every non-Christian friend is bad for them, and, perhaps as importantly, that every Christian friend is *good* for them. Of course try to steer your child away from harmful influences – but don't assume that someone is in that category just because they don't have a Christian faith. Allow your children to bring their non-Christian friends into your home. Make those friends welcome. Love them.

I know the problem. In fact, I can almost see the letters that some readers are thinking of penning right now. Of course there are dangers. And, yes, we can all think of young people whose lives were ruined by bad company. I have often thought that the biblical injunction: "If any of you lacks wisdom, you should ask God, who gives generously to all"[5] could have been written especially for parents – this is one of those times when we need it in buckets. We need that wisdom – not just so that our children may learn what it really means to be salt and light, but so that we can get them ready for the real world.

Youth leaders in the USA have a word for children who have spent all their lives within the Christian community – home, school, sports, college. They call them "lifers". They say that two things are often true of such young people: first, they often lack a sense of awe about the things of God, and, second, they have little hope of surviving in the first non-Christian environment they enter.

But, when all is said and done, we are still their parents. We have to make the nest as safe as we can and watch out for the predators that may sneak up the tree and hurt our fledglings. We need to be ready to flap our wings every time we sense a threat – and help our kids learn to spot those danger signs for themselves. If we don't protect them, who will?

Just don't forget to teach them to fly.

Chapter 14

Give Them a Vision

Sometimes I think we bore kids out of the kingdom. Jesus didn't do that with people – he challenged them. And he challenged all kinds of people in all kinds of ways. I sometimes wonder how long the disciple Peter would have lasted in a typical British church. He'd have fidgeted in the sermons, caused trouble in the youth club, and got six months behind with his daily reading notes.

I remember hearing George Verwer, the founder of Operation Mobilisation, speaking many years ago and saying that Peter spent a fair amount of his time as a disciple getting wet. The disciples are in a boat on Lake Galilee and suddenly they see a figure walking on the water. The other disciples cower in the boat, but Peter yells out to Jesus, "Lord, if it's you, tell me to come to you on the water."[1] It's almost as if he's back in the playground, saying, "Double-dare me to get out of this boat." Of course we all know how it ends: Peter practically drowns. But he did get out of the boat and – for a time – he walked on water!

And now it is after the resurrection. The disciples are depressed and they have gone back to their old job of fishing on the lake, but suddenly they see a figure on the shore. John says, "It's the master!" and soon the disciples are rowing for all they are worth to get to him. But not Peter; no – rowing is too slow for this one. Peter jumps into the water and swims for all he is worth towards the man who has changed his life.[2]

By the time he gets to the beach, Jesus has breakfast ready and then there ensues that incredible conversation between the Son of God and the fisherman. Peter had been a student of Jesus for just three years and if a school report had been written on him it would probably have said something like: "Peter is lively in class but must control himself more. Peter could do better."

You couldn't have blamed his teacher for being less than positive. In that short time he had spoiled a very spiritual time at the transfiguration with a silly comment, denied he ever knew Jesus, and chopped somebody's ear off with a sword. But Jesus doesn't refer to any of that. He says, "Peter, do you love me?" Jesus was concerned with Peter's *heart*. And then he gave Peter something.

It wasn't a list of ways in which he could improve as a follower of Jesus, or a seven-day plan of Torah readings (not that that would have been a bad thing). No, Jesus said to Peter: "Feed my sheep."[3]

If Peter was looking for an almighty challenge, he had found it!

I'll bet when Peter was a kid he fidgeted in synagogue. It wouldn't have surprised me to see a grey-bearded rabbi leading a fourteen-year-old Peter by the ear home to his father. But Jesus saw what Peter *could be*. And, against the odds, he accepted the challenge: Peter became the shepherd of the church.

We somehow have to stop boring the Peters and the Petras in our churches. That doesn't mean we have to pander to them, but we do have to find a way to get their attention. It could be by scaring the life out of them and offering to give them a place on a team from the church going into Rwanda. It could be asking them to help in the kids' club that works with the more challenging youngsters from the inner-city estate, or organizing the all-night car wash to raise money for the new building. But, whatever we do, we have to give them a vision. And we have to take risks with them.

We often limit the offerings of service that young people can do in church to things that appeal to only certain kinds of kid: we say they can sing or play in the worship band, lead the youth Bible study, or join us in our all-night prayer vigil. But not all kids are made the same. Some are not primarily thinkers or musicians or even pray-ers, but… *doers*.

Don't write those kids off too quickly. Time and time again Jesus commends the "doers" – those who cross the road to help the wounded, those who visit the prisons and feed the hungry. But so often we forget this, and as a result our churches are full of Peters who believe that they have nothing to give.

They have tried what the other kids do and think they are "rubbish" at it. They are about to leave church because they don't "fit". Fight to keep them! Get your most innovative businesspeople, your best youth workers, your visionaries in a room together and ask how, as a church, you can challenge the kids who just don't seem to fit the mould to follow Jesus.

A friend of mine was asked to speak to twelve young people who were attending a compulsory education course for children who had been excluded from school. He was given thirty minutes for his talk. As soon as he walked into the room he could see that these kids had not the slightest interest in listening to what he had to say. So he put aside the notes of his talk and said, "I want to offer you a deal: I will ask you two questions and you must answer them. It will only take two minutes to do that and when that's over you can leave if you want to." Twelve heads nodded to approve the deal.

"OK," said my friend, "here's the first question: What do you most want to do with your life? Let's start at the end of the row."

The twelve answers to the first question were varied. One said she'd like to be a hairdresser and another wanted to travel the world. One boy wanted to become a professional footballer, another to be a film-maker.

When all twelve had given their answers, my friend said, "And now for the second question. This time we'll start at the other end of the row. What have you done this week to get you a little nearer to reaching your goal?" Not one child had done a single thing.

My friend then said, "We agreed a deal and you've kept your part of it – you are free to go. But anyone who wants to stay can, and we'll talk about ways that you can begin to achieve your dream." Only two kids left. One of the ten who stayed was the one who wanted to be a film-maker. Within three months of that day he had made his first film with the help of the BBC.

When Jesus met Peter he knew he needed to say something that would inspire him. He needed to give

Peter something that he could *do*. So he said to the man who had spent almost all his life trying to catch fish: "How would you like to fish for people?"

That got his attention.

A Final Word

Thank you for the time you have given me. All authors need to remember never to take for granted the patience and perseverance of those who choose to read the books they write. I know that you won't agree with everything I have said – I wouldn't want you to. And I also know I have probably missed out a hundred issues that you would have liked me to address. But the message of the book is simply this: every child is unique and every child is special. God knows them and loves them even more than you do, and he can do abundantly more in their lives than you could ever imagine.

Of course we often feel failures as parents and of course we are tempted to believe that if we had another chance we'd do it all so differently. But so often these thoughts are guilt trips that we would do well to lay down. Good parents sometimes have children who break their hearts and, although none of us can change the past, we can all pray. God is a God of change and redemption and when we cry out to him for help as a parent, he has a power so great it can negate all our mistakes and foolishness.

Let's not judge each other by how we think our children are doing. Let's not live our lives wondering what other Christians are making of our parenting. And don't ever give up hope as a parent, a youth worker or a church leader. Try to remember that God looks at the heart.

You cannot bear the responsibility of whether the kids that you care about decide to follow Christ – that is too heavy a burden to bear. There are many burdens we *are* called to bear as parents, but this is not one of them. Remember that God has no grandchildren – it is their decision.

But you and I can, with God's help and realizing our frailty, try to live lives at home and in church that will make their hearts more likely to be soft towards him. And we can pray for them. We must – for we all know that, even if we achieve it, the title of this book is not enough – not nearly enough. We are their parents and we have a much greater goal for our children.

We want them to *love* him.

Notes

Introduction

1. Wayne Cordeiro, *Leading on Empty: Refilling Your Tank and Renewing Your Passion*, Grand Rapids: Bethany House Publishers, 2009.
2. John White, *Parents in Pain – Help and Hope for Troubled Families*, IVP, 1988.
3. C. S. Lewis, *The Four Loves*, HarperCollins (reissue), 2002.
4. Joel 2:25.

Chapter 1: God has No Grandchildren

1. Proverbs 22:6.
2. John 1:29.
3. Luke 7:20.
4. Luke 7:28.

Chapter 3: Don't Sweat the Small Stuff

1. Matthew 25:31–46.
2. Matthew 23:23.

Chapter 5: Over-busyness

1. John 6:15.
2. Luke 12:13–14.
3. Luke 4:42–44.
4. Ecclesiastes 4:4.
5. Henri J. M. Nouwen, *The Genesee Diary: Report from a Trappist Monastery*, London: Darton, Longman & Todd Ltd, 1995.

Chapter 7: Hypocrisy

1. Eugene Peterson, *Living the Message: Daily Help for Living the God-Centered Life*, San Francisco: HarperOne, 2007.
2. Matthew 23:13 (*The Message*).
3. David Kinnaman and Gabe Lyons, *unChristian: What a Generation Really Thinks About Christianity and Why it Matters*, Grand Rapids: Baker Books, 2007.
4. Charles Haddon Spurgeon, *Commentary on Matthew*, Matthew 5:14–15, http://grace-ebooks.com [accessed 4 February 2010].

Chapter 8: Judgmentalism

1. David Kinnaman and Gabe Lyons, *unChristian: What a Generation Really Thinks About Christianity and Why it Matters*, Grand Rapids: Baker Books, 2007.
2. David Kinnaman and Gabe Lyons, *unChristian: What a Generation Really Thinks About Christianity and Why it Matters*, Grand Rapids: Baker Books, 2007.
3. David Kinnaman and Gabe Lyons, *unChristian: What a Generation Really Thinks About Christianity and Why it Matters*, Grand Rapids: Baker Books, 2007.
4. Romans 1:18.
5. Romans 2:1, 4 (NLT).
6. David Kinnaman and Gabe Lyons, *unChristian: What a Generation Really Thinks About Christianity and Why it Matters*, Grand Rapids: Baker Books, 2007.
7. Philip Yancey, *What's So Amazing About Grace?*, Grand Rapids: Zondervan, 1997.
8. Matthew 7:1–2.

Chapter 9: Overfamiliarity

1. Matthew 13:58 (author's paraphrase).
2. Matthew 13:54–57 (author's paraphrase).
3. Paul Scanlon, *The Battle for the Loins*, Bradford: Abundant Life Publishing, 2004.
4. Paul Scanlon, *The Battle for the Loins*, Bradford: Abundant Life Publishing, 2004.

Chapter 10: Get Them Ready for Disappointment with Others

1. John 13:34–35 (author's paraphrase).
2. James 1:17 (author's paraphrase).

Chapter 11: Get Them Ready for Disappointment with Themselves

1. Lynne Hybels, *Nice Girls Don't Change the World*, Grand Rapids: Zondervan, 2005.
2. Galatians 3:3.
3. Max Lucado, *Just Like Jesus*, Thomas Nelson, 2001.
4. 1 John 3:20 (author's paraphrase).

Chapter 12: Get Them Ready for Disappointment with God

1. Habakkuk 3:17–18.
2. Daniel 3:17–18.
3. Luke 22:42.
4. Matthew 26:42 (author's paraphrase).
5. Hebrews 11:33–35 (author's paraphrase).
6. Hebrews 11:35–36 (author's paraphrase).

Chapter 13: Get Them Ready for the Real World

1. Jack Schreur and Jerry Schreur, *Family Fears*, Wheaton: Victor Books, 1994.
2. "The Day the World Shuts Down", *Newsweek*, June 1997.
3. Matthew 6:25–27.
4. Leviticus 26:36.
5. James 1:5 (author's paraphrase).

Chapter 14: Give Them a Vision

1. Matthew 14:28.
2. John 21:7.
3. John 21:15–17.

Afterword

More information and support

This book is part of the work of the charity Care for the Family, founded by Rob Parsons. Our aim is to strengthen family life and help those who are hurting because of family difficulties.

Go to www.careforthefamily.org.uk where you can:
- Sign up for your free bi-monthly email newsletter, with helpful articles and tips for your family life

- Find out about events near you

- Read articles and discover more resources

- Find specialist support for many family situations including bereaved parents, stepfamilies and more

www.careforthefamily.org.uk
(029) 2081 0800
Care for the Family
Garth House
Leon Avenue
Cardiff CF15 7RG

Please tell us your thoughts!

Go to www.gettingyourkidsthroughchurch.org.uk/ survey/kids to share your views

- Was this book helpful to you?
- Have you faced particular challenges as you bring up your kids in church?
- Do you have tips or ideas to share from your experiences?

This book is only part of the project *Getting Your Kids Through Church Without Them Ending Up Hating God*. We are hoping to develop a study guide, website and other resources for parents, church leaders, children's and youth workers.

We'd love to hear from you – your feedback, ideas and experiences will help us as we develop these resources.

Simply go to www.gettingyourkidsthroughchurch. org.uk/survey/kids to answer a few questions about the book, and to share your experiences. Thank you so much!

Care for the Family

BRINGING HOME THE
PRODIGALS

This simple parable has been called the greatest short story in the world. It is the tale of the boy who broke his father's heart and yet could not destroy the love the father had for him. And although it's over 2,000 years old, it speaks to us today with the promise of new beginnings, the triumph of love and forgiveness, the joy of reconciliation, and the call to the church to be ready when our prodigals return.

The *Bringing Home the Prodigals* combined book and DVD pack will give you a new perspective on the story of the prodigal son as Rob Parsons shares his passion for prodigals.

Including:

- Always leave a light on
- Making prodigals of those that never were
- Struggling with guilt we were never meant to carry
- The life-changing power of forgiveness
- The danger of meeting the elder brother first
- Praying the prodigals home

ROB PARSONS
Bringing Home the Prodigals
'This book is a gift to the whole Church'
DR R.T. KENDALL

PRODIGALS
Preparing for our prodigals' return

Pack price
£9.99

"This book is a gift to the whole church" Dr RT Kendall

Find out more at **www.careforthefamily.co.uk/prodigals**
or by calling **(029) 2081 0800**

Care for the Family - A Christian response to a world of need.
A Registered Charity (England and Wales: 1066905; Scotland: SC038497).

'Elegantly and compellingly written, with both sensitivity and humour.'
Ned Temko, The Observer

'Reading this may be the best 60 minutes you will ever spend.'
Suzie Hayman,
BBC radio agony aunt

10 practical ways to transform your family life – for the better

'I would recommend this book to anyone, whatever their family circumstance.'
Jeremy Todd,
Chief Executive, Parentline Plus

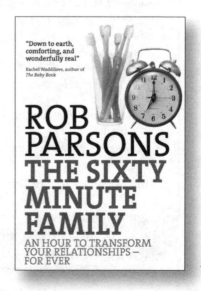

"Down to earth, comforting, and wonderfully real"
Rachel Waddilove, author of
The Baby Book

ROB PARSONS
THE SIXTY MINUTE FAMILY
AN HOUR TO TRANSFORM YOUR RELATIONSHIPS – FOR EVER

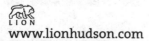
LION
www.lionhudson.com